8/22

THE
TERROR FACTORY

THE TERROR FACTORY

INSIDE THE FBI'S MANUFACTURED
WAR ON TERRORISM

TREVOR AARONSON

PUBLISHING

BROOKLYN, NEW YORK

Printed in the United States of America
10 9 8 7 6 5 4 3 2 1

Ig Publishing
392 Clinton Avenue
Brooklyn, NY 11238
www.igpub.com

Library of Congress Cataloging-in-Publication Data

Aaronson, Trevor.
  The terror factory : inside the FBI's manufactured war on terrorism / Trevor Aaronson.
     pages cm
  Includes bibliographical references.
  ISBN 978-1-935439-61-5
  1. United States. Federal Bureau of Investigation. 2. Terrorism-- United States--Prevention. 3. Undercover operations--Moral and ethical aspects--United States. 4. Intelligence service--Moral and ethical aspects--United States. I. Title.
  HV8144.F43A23 2013
  363.25'9--dc23
                                        2012043238

Perhaps it is a universal truth that the loss of liberty at home is to be charged against provisions against danger, real or pretended, from abroad. — James Madison, 1798

CONTENTS

INTRODUCTION

Michael Curtis Reynolds was unemployed and living in his elderly mother's house in Wilkes-Barre, Pennsylvania, when he became a government-manufactured terrorist.

At forty-seven years of age, Reynolds was a drifter with a bad employment history and a worse credit report. In addition, his behavior over several decades suggested that his grip on reality was tenuous at best. In 1978, for example, he tried to blow up his parents' house in Purdys, New York, wiring gasoline, cans of paint, and propane to a timed ignition device. The improvised bomb failed to ignite the propane and merely started a small fire. Reynolds pleaded guilty to attempted arson.[1]

Reynolds got married in 1982 and fathered three children. His father-in-law, Richard Danise, despite not approving of the marriage, tried to help his daughter Tammy and Reynolds start a life together, giving them an acre of land and signing for a mortgage to finance the construction of a home. But Reynolds couldn't reconcile the reality of his average life with the fantasy of his outsized ideas. "He literally wanted to build a castle, with turrets and everything else," Danise remembered.[2] The house was never built, and Tammy divorced Reynolds, getting full custody of their children.

Reynolds was a man on the margins, bouncing around from place to place, job to job. In 2005, outraged by the war in Iraq and living in his mother's house in Pennsylvania, Reynolds logged in to a Yahoo forum called OBLCrew—OBL for Osama bin Laden—and shared his dream of bombing the Trans-Alaska Pipeline. He needed assistance, he told the forum members. No one responded. Reynolds followed up the next day. "Still awaiting someone serious about contact. Would be a pity to lose this idea," he wrote.

The following day, a person claiming to be an Al Qaeda operative responded and offered $40,000 to fund the attack, which evolved into a plan to fill trucks with explosives and bomb oil refineries in New Jersey and Wyoming, as well as the Trans-Alaska Pipeline. They arranged to meet at a rest stop on Interstate 15 in Idaho, where Reynolds believed that he'd collect the $40,000 and move forward with his ambitious plan. But Reynolds didn't know that his supposed Al Qaeda contact with money to burn was an FBI informant. On December 5, 2005, Reynolds arrived at the rest stop only to be greeted by FBI agents.[3] At the time of his arrest, Reynolds had less than twenty-five dollars to his name. Eventually, he was tried and convicted of providing material support to Al Qaeda and received thirty years in prison. "Because of the astute work of the FBI, the diabolical plans of a would-be Al Qaeda sympathizer were uncovered," Pennsylvania U.S. Attorney Thomas A. Marino said in a statement following Reynolds's conviction. "Individuals such as Reynolds represent a threat to our safety. I commend the FBI and everyone involved in the prosecution of this case for bringing him to justice."

Despite his conviction, was Reynolds a dangerous terrorist? The answer is no—he was a troubled man unlikely to escape the fringes of society. He talked big and had a history of doing stupid things. He was unemployed, broke ,and living with his mother at middle age, a caricature of the all-American loser. But an informant posing as an Al Qaeda operative offered him more money than he had ever seen at one time in his entire life and overnight he became a "threat to our safety."

For years, as an investigative reporter with newspapers, I couldn't help but notice how the U.S. government was putting forward to the public people who seemed to have become terrorists only as a result of the prodding and inducements of FBI informants and undercover agents. In most of these cases, the defendants appeared to be sad sacks like Michael Curtis Reynolds—individuals with no capacity to do any significant harm if left to their own devices—and it was FBI informants who provided the ideas, the means, and the opportunities for horrific plots involving the bombings of government buildings and office towers, synagogues, and public transit systems. Curious, I began pulling court records about these cases and documenting which ones involved defendants who, like Reynolds, had no actual contacts with terrorist organizations and were lured into their plots by FBI informants. A provocative question underpinned my research: How many so-called terrorists prosecuted in U.S. courts since 9/11 were real terrorists? I wanted to do a systematic analysis of all terrorism cases since September 11, 2001, to answer this question, but I hit an early roadblock: While the U.S. Department of Justice tracked terrorism prosecutions internally, this data was not made public. I needed to know exactly which cases the Justice Department considered terrorism-related, and so I needed this internal data—which was impossible to obtain without someone leaking it from the inside.

Ironically, it was Khalid Sheikh Mohammed, the Kuwaiti-born mastermind of the 9/11 attacks, who was responsible for my lucky break. After his capture in Pakistan in 2003, Mohammed had been sent to the U.S. detention facility at Guantanamo Bay Naval Base in Cuba. In November 2009, U.S. Attorney General Eric Holder decided that the Justice Department would prosecute Mohammed and four others involved in planning the 9/11 attacks at the U.S. District Court in Manhattan. Citing concerns about public safety and the handling of potentially classified information during a trial that would be open to the public, Congress questioned the wisdom of putting the 9/11 mastermind on trial on U.S. soil. Holder appeared before Congress in March 2010 to assure the public that the Justice Department was not only capable of providing a secure and fair setting for the trial, but also was well accomplished in prosecuting terrorists. To prove the latter, the attorney general provided a document containing nearly nine years' worth of the very data I needed—a list of about 400 people whom the Justice Department had prosecuted in the United States since 9/11 and considered terrorists.

The document explained clearly, and for the first time publicly, how the Justice Department determined whether a particular defendant was a terrorist. The government seg-regated terrorism offenses into two categories. Category I included the kind of offenses you would typically associate with terrorism, such as aircraft sabotage, hostage taking, and providing material support to terrorists. Category II offenses could be any federal crime in the United States, including lower-level felony offenses such as an immigration violation or lying to an FBI agent, committed by someone who had a link, however oblique, to international terrorism. For the first time, I had a government data set that could form the basis of a systematic analysis of terrorism prosecutions since 9/11 and a formula to use in determining whether future cases fit the Justice Department's terrorism criteria. How many of the defendants posed actual threats, based on the evidence? How many of the prosecutions involved FBI sting operations using informants? How many of those informants played such an active role in the investigation that they reasonably could be described as agents provocateurs? Those were just some of the questions I wanted to answer, and the data Attorney General Holder and the Justice Department provided represented only the beginning. For every case, I would need to pore over hundreds, if not thousands, of pages of court records to answer those questions. I would also need to add and analyze defendants whose cases met the Justice Department's criteria for terrorism but were announced after Holder released his document in March 2010.

The cost of and time needed for this type of investigation seemed staggering, and I had about as much capacity to do it on my own as Michael Curtis Reynolds had on his own of bombing the Trans-Alaska Pipeline. While I had some early research funding from the Carnegie Legal Reporting Fellowship at Syracuse University and the Fund for Investigative Journalism, I knew I needed about a year to build and analyze the database and then meet with enough current and former FBI officials to help me understand what the data meant. I pitched this ambitious project to the University of California Berkeley's Investigative Reporting Program, run by Lowell Bergman, a Pulitzer Prize–winning journalist and former *60 Minutes* producer. Bergman's IRP had funded ambitious projects that examined in recent years, among other things, death investigations in the United States and the connections between U.S.-based casino companies and organized crime in Macau.

Bergman took a gamble on my project in the fall of 2010. For several months inside an office across the street from the Berkeley Graduate School of Journalism, I worked with a research assistant, Lauren Ellis, to examine closely court records from every case on the Justice Department's list as well as from every subsequent case that fit the government's criteria for terrorism. From these examinations we built a database that provided fields for whether an informant was used, the name of the informant, the role of the informant, and notes to explain how cases were connected, particularly through the use of the same informant. It was painstaking, time-consuming work. While the Justice Department discloses when the FBI uses informants, it doesn't advertise their use. There's no check box, no single place in the court file where the Justice Department reports whether the FBI used an informant in its investigation. Lauren and I had to read through thousands of pages of court records to find the information. Sometimes, confirmation of the government's use of an informant was easy to locate—it would be mentioned on the first page of the criminal affidavit, one of the first documents prosecutors file when bringing charges. Other times, confirmation of an informant's presence would be buried in a defense lawyer's motion or wouldn't come up until the trial.

But we didn't stop there. A primary part of what we wanted to document was how the FBI used an informant in a terrorism case. Did the informant just provide a tip that the FBI acted on, as you might expect an informant to do? Or did he play a more active role, such as in a sting operation? And if the informant was in a sting operation, was he—like the informant in the case of Michael Curtis Reynolds—an agent provocateur, providing the means and opportunity to an individual who had no capacity on his own for terrorism? Looking closely at each case, we could determine this, and then document it systematically.

By August 2011, with nearly ten years of terrorism prosecutions since 9/11, we had a database of 508 defendants whom the U.S. government considered terrorists. The way the data broke down was illuminating. Of the 508 defendants, 243 had been targeted through an FBI informant, 158 had been caught in an FBI terrorism sting, and 49 had encountered an agent provocateur. Most of the people who didn't face off against an informant weren't directly involved with terrorism at all, but were instead Category II offenders, small-time criminals with distant links to terrorists overseas. Seventy-two of these Category II offenders had been charged with making false statements, while 121 had been prosecuted for immigration violations. Of the 508 cases, I could count on one hand the number of actual terrorists, such as failed New York City subway bomber Najibullah Zazi, who posed a direct and immediate threat to the United States.

While building the terrorism database, I spent a lot of time in New York and Washington, D.C., interviewing current and former FBI agents in an effort to understand what was going on at the Bureau and what the story was behind the data. I also pulled state court records in cities including New York, Los Angeles, and Miami in an attempt to reveal the full tales of the men—most of them criminals themselves—identified as informants in FBI sting operations. Lowell Bergman and I presented our findings to *Mother Jones*, which agreed to sign on as a full partner, devoting a cover story and substantial resources to make my database accessible and searchable online, as well as providing the fact-checking manpower to make sure that everything, from the data to the story, was correct and confirmed.

What became clear from my reporting is that in the decade since 9/11, the FBI has built the largest network of spies ever to exist in the United States—with ten times as many informants on the streets today as there were during the infamous Cointelpro operations under FBI director J. Edgar Hoover—with the majority of these spies focused on ferreting out terrorism in Muslim communities. The *Mother Jones* story revealed for the first time the inner workings of the FBI's informant program and how agents provocateurs were behind most of the scary terrorist plots you've heard about since 9/11. But after that story was published, I couldn't help but think about all of the material I had that didn't make it into the article—the rich history of how the FBI transformed into something of a domestic CIA, the inside stories of dozens of terrorism sting operations, interviews with current and former FBI agents I'd met during my reporting, and the full explanation of how the government has exaggerated the threat of Islamic terrorism in the United States. I believe the FBI's use of terrorism stings is one of the most important national security stories of the last decade, and a desire to tell that story in full, and in as much detail I could, led me to write this book.

For more than a decade, the FBI has thrown as much as it can toward an effort to stop the "next" terrorist attack. Every year, the U.S. government allocates $3 billion to the FBI to prevent the next 9/11, more money than the Bureau receives to combat organized crime. But what an analysis of ten years' worth of Justice Department data shows is that Islamic terrorism in the United States is not an immediate and dangerous threat. The FBI's thousands of informants and billions of dollars have not resulted in the capture of dozens of killers ready and able to bomb a crowded building or gun down people in a suburban shopping mall. Instead, the FBI's trawling in Muslim communities has resulted largely in sting operations that target easily susceptible men on the margins of society, men like Michael Curtis Reynolds. Since 9/11, the FBI and the Justice Department have labeled as terrorists a mentally troubled man who worked at Walmart, a video game store clerk whose only valuable possession was a set of stereo speakers, a university student who was about to be evicted from his apartment, and a window washer who had dropped out of college, among others. All of these men were involved in FBI terrorism stings in which an informant came up with the idea and provided the necessary means and opportunity for the terrorist plot. While we have captured a few terrorists since 9/11, we have manufactured many more.

1. TERROR TRAPS

Antonio Martinez was a punk. The twenty-two-year-old from Baltimore was chunky, with a wide nose and jet-black hair pulled back close to his scalp and tied into long braids that hung past his shoulders. He preferred to be called Muhammad Hussain, the name he gave himself following his conversion to Islam. But his mother still called him Tony, and she couldn't understand her son's burning desire to be the Maryland Mujahideen.

As a young man, Martinez had been angry and lost. He'd dropped out of Laurel High School, in Prince George's County, Maryland, and spent his teens as a small-time thief in the Washington, D.C., suburbs. By the age of sixteen, he'd been charged with armed robbery. In February 2008, at the age of eighteen, he tried to steal a car. Catholic University doctoral student Daniel Tobin was looking out of the window of his apartment one day when he saw a man driving off in his car. Tobin gave chase, running between apartment buildings and finally catching up to the stolen vehicle. He opened the passenger-side door and got in. Martinez, in the driver's seat, dashed out and ran away on foot. Jumping behind the wheel, Tobin followed the would-be car thief. "You may as well give up running," he yelled at Martinez.[1] Martinez was apprehended and charged with grand theft of a motor vehicle—he had stolen the vehicle using an extra set of car keys which had gone missing when someone had broken into Tobin's apartment earlier. However, prosecutors dropped the charges against Martinez after Tobin failed to appear in court.

Despite the close call, Martinez's petty crimes continued. One month after the car theft, he and a friend approached a cashier at a Safeway grocery store, acting as if they wanted to buy potato chips. When the cashier opened the register, Martinez and his friend grabbed as much money as they could and ran out of the store. The cashier and store manager chased after them, and later identified the pair to police. Martinez pleaded guilty to theft of one hundred dollars and received a ninety-day suspended sentence, plus six months of probation.

Searching for greater meaning in his life, Martinez was baptized and became a Christian when he was twenty-one years old, but he didn't stick with the religion. "He said he tried the Christian thing. He just really didn't understand it," said Alisha Legrand, a former girlfriend.[2] Martinez chose Islam instead. On his Facebook page, Martinez wrote that he was "just a yung brotha from the wrong side of the tracks who embraced Islam."[3] But for reasons that have never been clear to his family and friends, Martinez drifted toward a violent, extremist brand of Islam. When the FBI discovered him, Martinez was an angry extremist mouthing off on Facebook about violence, with misspelled posts such as, "The sword is cummin the reign of oppression is about 2 cease inshallah." Based on the Facebook postings alone, an FBI agent gave an informant the "green light" to get to know Martinez and determine if he had a propensity for violence. In other words, to see if he was dangerous.

The government was setting the trap.

On the evening of December 2, 2010, Martinez was in another Muslim's car as they drove through Baltimore. A hidden device recorded their conversation. His mother had called, and Martinez had just finished talking to her on his cell phone. He was aggravated. "She wants me to be like everybody else, being in school, working," he told his friend. "For me, it's different. I have this zeal for deen and she doesn't understand that."[4] Martinez's mother didn't know that her son had just left a meeting with a purported Afghan-born terrorist who had agreed to provide him with a car bomb. But she wasn't the only one in the dark that night. Martinez himself didn't know his new terrorist friend was an undercover agent with the Federal Bureau of Investigation and that the man driving the car—a man he'd met only a few weeks earlier—was a paid informant for federal law enforcement.

Five days later, Martinez met again with the man he believed to be a terrorist. The informant was there, too. They were all, Martinez believed, brothers in arms and in Islam. In a parking lot near the Armed Forces Career Center on Baltimore National Pike, Martinez, the informant, and the undercover FBI agent piled into an SUV, where the undercover agent showed Martinez the device that would detonate the car bomb and how to use it. He then unveiled to the twenty-two-year-old the bomb in the back of the SUV and demonstrated what he'd need to do to activate it. "I'm ready, man," Martinez said. "It ain't like you seein' it on the news. You gonna be there. You gonna hear the bomb go off. You gonna be, uh, shooting, gettin' shot at. It's gonna be real. ... I'm excited, man."[5]

That night, Martinez, who had little experience behind the wheel of a car, needed to practice driving the SUV around the empty parking lot. Once he felt comfortable doing what most teenagers can do easily, Martinez and his associates devised a plan: Martinez would park the bomb-on-wheels in the parking lot outside the military recruiting center. One of his associates would then pick him up, and they'd drive together to a vantage point where Martinez could detonate the bomb and delight in the resulting chaos and carnage.

The next morning, the three men put their plan into action. Martinez hopped into the SUV and activated the bomb, as he'd been instructed, and then drove to the military recruiting station. He parked right in front. The informant, trailing in another car, picked up Martinez and drove him to the vantage point, just as planned. Everything was falling into place, and Martinez was about to launch his first attack in what he hoped would be for him a lifetime of jihad against the only nation he had ever known.

Looking out at the military recruiting station, Martinez lifted the detonation device and triggered the bomb. Smiling, he watched expectantly. Nothing happened. Suddenly, FBI agents rushed in and arrested the man they'd later identify in court records as "Antonio Martinez a/k/a Muhammad Hussain." Federal prosecutors in Maryland charged Martinez with attempted murder of federal officers and attempted use of a weapon of mass destruction. He faced at least thirty-five years in prison if convicted at trial.

"This is not Tony," a woman identifying herself as Martinez's mother told a reporter after the arrest. "I think he was brainwashed with that Islam crap."[6] Joseph Balter, a federal public defender, told the court during a detention hearing that FBI agents had entrapped Martinez, whom he referred to by his chosen name. The terrorist plot was, Balter said, "the creation of the government—a creation which was implanted into Mr. Hussain's mind." He added: "There was nothing provided which showed that Mr. Hussain had any ability whatsoever to carry out any kind of plan."[7]

Despite Balter's claims, a little more than a year after his indictment, Martinez chose not to challenge the government's charges in court. On January 26, 2012, Martinez dropped his entrapment defense and pleaded guilty to attempted use of a weapon of mass destruction under a deal that will require him to serve twenty-five years in prison—more years than he's been alive. Neither Martinez nor Balter would comment on the reasons they chose a plea agreement, though in a sentencing hearing, Balter told the judge he believed the entire case could have been avoided had the FBI counseled, rather than encouraged, Martinez.

The U.S. Department of Justice touted the conviction as another example of the government keeping citizens safe from terrorists. "We are catching dangerous suspects before they strike, and we are investigating them in a way that maximizes the liberty and security of law-abiding citizens," U.S. attorney for the District of Maryland Rod J. Rosenstein said in a statement announcing Martinez's plea agreement. "That is what the American people expect of the Justice Department, and that is what we aim to deliver."[8] Indeed, that is exactly what the Justice Department and the Federal Bureau of Investigation have been delivering throughout the decade since the attacks of September 11, 2001. But whether it's what the American people expect is questionable, because most Americans today have no idea that since 9/11, one single organization has been responsible for hatching and financing more terrorist plots in the United States than any other. That organization isn't Al Qaeda, the terrorist network founded by Osama bin Laden and responsible for the spectacular 2001 attacks on New York's World Trade Center and the Pentagon in Washington, D.C. And it isn't Lashkar-e-Taiba, Jaish-e-Mohammed, Al-Shabaab, Hamas, Palestinian Islamic Jihad, or any of the other more than forty U.S.-designated foreign terrorist organizations. No, the organization responsible for more terrorist plots over the last decade than any other is the FBI. Through elaborate and expensive sting operations involving informants and undercover agents posing as terrorists, the FBI has arrested and the Justice Department has prosecuted dozens of men government officials say posed direct—but by no means immediate or credible—threats to the United States.

Just as in the Martinez case, in terrorism sting after terrorism sting, FBI and DOJ officials have hosted high-profile press conferences to announce yet another foiled terrorist plot. But what isn't publicized during these press conferences is the fact that government-described terrorists such as Antonio Martinez were able to carry forward with their potentially lethal plots only because FBI informants and agents provided them with all of the means—in most cases delivering weapons and equipment, in some cases even paying for rent and doling out a little spending money to keep targets on the hook. In cities around the country where terrorism sting operations have occurred—among them New York City, Albany, Chicago, Miami, Baltimore, Portland, Tampa, Houston, and Dallas—a central question exists: Is the FBI catching terrorists or creating them?

In the years since the attacks of September 11, 2001, the federal law enforcement profile of a terrorist has changed dramatically. The men responsible for downing the World Trade Center were disciplined and patient; they were also living and training in the United States with money from an

Al Qaeda cell led by Kuwaiti-born Khalid Sheikh Mohammad. In the days and weeks following 9/11, federal officials anxiously awaited a second wave of attacks, which would be launched, they believed at the time, by several sleeper cells around the country. But the feared second wave never crashed ashore. Instead, the United States and allied nations invaded Afghanistan, Al Qaeda's home base, and forced Osama bin Laden and his deputies into hiding. Bruised and hunted, Al Qaeda no longer had the capability to train terrorists and send them to the United States.

In response, Al Qaeda's leaders moved to what FBI officials describe as a "franchise model." If you can't run Al Qaeda as a hierarchal, centrally organized outfit, the theory went, run it as a franchise. In other words, export ideas— not terrorists. Al Qaeda and its affiliated organizations went online, setting up websites and forums dedicated to instilling their beliefs in disenfranchised Muslims already living in Western nations. A slickly designed magazine, appropriately titled *Inspire*, quickly followed. Article headlines included "I Am Proud to Be a Traitor to America,"[9] and "Why Did I Choose Al-Qaeda?"[10] Anwar al-Awlaki, the American-born, high-ranking Al Qaeda official who was killed in a U.S. drone strike in Yemen on September 30, 2011, became something of the terrorist organization's Dear Abby. Have a question about Islam? Ask Anwar! Muslim men in nations throughout the Western world would email him questions, and al-Awlaki would reply dutifully, and in English, encouraging many of his electronic pen pals to violent action. Al-Awlaki also kept a blog and a Facebook page, and regularly posted recruitment videos to YouTube. He said in one video:

> I specifically invite the youth to either fight in the West or join their brothers in the fronts of jihad: Afghanistan, Iraq, and Somalia.
>
> I invite them to join us in our new front, Yemen, the base from which the great jihad of the Arabian Peninsula will begin, the base from which the greatest army of Islam will march forth.[11]

Al Qaeda's move to a franchise model met with some success. U.S. army major Nadal Hassan, for example, corresponded with al-Awlaki before he killed thirteen people and wounded twenty-nine others in the Fort Hood, Texas, shootings in 2009.[12] Antonio Martinez and other American-born men, many of them recent converts to Islam, also sent al-Awlaki messages or watched Al Qaeda propaganda videos online before moving forward in alleged terrorist plots.

The FBI has a term for Martinez and other alleged terrorists like him: *lone wolf*. Officials at the Bureau now believe that the next terrorist attack will likely come from a lone wolf, and this belief is at the core of a federal law enforcement policy known variously as *preemption*, *prevention*, and *disruption*. FBI counterterrorism agents want to catch terrorists *before* they act, and to accomplish this, federal law enforcement officials have in the decade since 9/11 created the largest domestic spying network ever to exist in the United States. In fact, the FBI today has ten times as many informants as it did in the 1960s, when former FBI director J. Edgar Hoover made the Bureau infamous for inserting spies into organizations as varied as Reverend Dr. Martin Luther King Jr.'s and the Ku Klux Klan. Modern FBI informants aren't burrowing into political groups, however; they are focused on terrorism, on identifying today the terrorist of tomorrow, and U.S. government officials acknowledge that while terrorist threats do exist from domestic organizations, such as white supremacist groups and the sovereign citizen movement, they believe the greatest threat comes from within U.S. Muslim communities due, in large part, to the aftereffects of the shock and awe Al Qaeda delivered on September 11, 2001.

The FBI's vast army of spies, located in every community in the United States with enough Muslims to support a mosque, has one primary function: to identify the next lone wolf. According to the Bureau, a lone wolf is likely to be a single male age sixteen to thirty-five. Therefore, informants and their FBI handlers are on the lookout for young Muslims who espouse radical beliefs, are vocal about their disapproval of U.S. foreign policy, or have expressed sympathy for international terrorist groups. If they find anyone who meets the criteria, they move him to the next stage: the sting, in which an FBI informant, posing as a terrorist, offers to help facilitate a terrorist attack for the target.

On a cold February morning in 2011, I met with Peter Ahearn, a retired FBI special agent who directed the Western New York Joint Terrorism Task Force, in a coffee shop outside Washington, D.C., to talk about how the FBI runs its operations. Ahearn was among the Bureau's vanguard as it transformed into a counterterrorism organization in the wake of 9/11. An average-built man with a small dimple on his chin and close-cropped brown hair receding in the front, Ahearn oversaw one of the earliest post-9/11 terrorism investigations, involving the so-called Lackawanna Six—a group of six Yemeni-American men living outside Buffalo, New York, who attended a training camp in Afghanistan and were convicted of providing material support to Al Qaeda. "If you're doing a sting right, you're offering the target multiple chances to back out," Ahearn told me. "Real people don't say, 'Yeah, let's go bomb that place.' Real people call the cops."

Indeed, while terrorism sting operations are a new practice for the Bureau, they are an evolution of an FBI tactic that has for decades captured the imaginations of Hollywood filmmakers. In 1982, as the illegal drug trade overwhelmed local police resources nationwide and contributed to an increase in violent crime, President Ronald Reagan's first attorney general, William French Smith, gave the FBI jurisdiction over federal drug crimes, which previously had been the exclusive domain of the U.S. Drug Enforcement Administration. Eager to show up their DEA rivals, FBI agents began aggressively sending undercover agents into America's cities. This was relatively new territory for the FBI, which, during Hoover's thirty-seven-year stewardship, had mandated that agents wear a suit and tie at all times, federal law enforcement badge easily accessible from the coat pocket. But an increasingly powerful Mafia and the bloody drug war compelled the FBI to begin enforcing federal laws from the street level. In searching for drug crimes, FBI agents hunted sellers as well as buyers, and soon learned one of the best strategies was to become part of the action.

Most people have no doubt seen drug sting operations as portrayed in countless movies and television shows. At its most cliché, the scene is set in a Miami high-rise apartment, its floor-to-ceiling windows overlooking the cresting waves of the Atlantic Ocean. There's a man seated at the dining table; he's longhaired, with a scruffy face, and he has a briefcase next to him. But that's not all. Hidden on the other side of the room is a camera making a grainy black-and-white recording of the entire scene. The apartment's door swings open and two men saunter in, the camera recording their every move and word. Everyone sits down at the table. The two men hand over bundles of cash. The scruffy man then hands over the briefcase. The two guests of course expect to find cocaine inside. Instead, the briefcase is empty, and as soon as they open it to find the drugs missing, FBI agents rush in, guns drawn for the takedown. Federal law enforcement officials call this type of sting operation a "no-dope bust," and it has been an effective tool for decades. It's also the direct predecessor to today's terrorism sting. Instead of empty briefcases, the FBI today uses inert bombs and disabled assault rifles, and now that counter-terrorism is the Bureau's top priority, the investigation of major drug crimes has largely fallen back to the DEA. Just as no-dope busts resulted in the arrest and prosecution of those in the drug trade in the twentieth century, terrorism sting operations are resulting in the arrest and prosecution of would-be terrorists in this century.

While the assumptions behind drug stings and terrorism stings are similar, there is a fundamental flaw in the assumption underpinning the latter. In drug stings, federal law enforcement officials assume that any buyer caught in a sting would have been able to buy or sell drugs elsewhere had that buyer not fallen into the FBI trap. The numbers support this assumption. In 2010, the most recent year for which data is available, the DEA seized 29,179 kilograms, or 64,328 pounds, of cocaine in the United States.[13] Likewise, in terrorism stings, federal law enforcement officials assume that any would-be terrorists caught in a sting would have been able to acquire the means elsewhere to carry out their violent plans had they not been ensnared by the FBI. The problem with this assumption is that no data exists to support it, and what data is available suggests would-be Islamic terrorists caught in FBI terrorism stings never could have obtained the capability to carry out their planned violent acts were it not for the FBI's assistance.

In the ten years following 9/11, the FBI and the Justice Department indicted and convicted more than 150 people following sting operations involving alleged connections to international terrorism. Few of these defendants had any connection to terrorists, evidence showed, and those who did have connections, however tangential, never had the capacity to launch attacks on their own. In fact, of the more than 150 terrorism sting operation defendants, an FBI informant not only led one of every three terrorist plots, but also provided all the necessary weapons, money, and transportation.[14]

The FBI's logic to support the use of terrorism stings goes something like this: By catching a lone wolf before he strikes, federal law enforcement can take him off the streets before he meets a real terrorist who can provide him with weapons and munitions. However, to this day, no example exists of a lone wolf, by himself unable to launch an attack, becoming operational through meeting an actual terrorist in the United States. In addition, in the dozens of terrorism sting operations since 9/11, the would-be terrorists are usually uneducated, unsophisticated, and economically desperate—not the attributes of someone likely to plan and launch a sophisticated, violent attack without significant help.

This isn't to say there have not been deadly and potentially deadly terrorist attacks and threats in the United States since 9/11. Hesham Mohamed Hadayet, an Egyptian, opened fire on the El Al ticket counter at Los Angeles International Airport on July 4, 2002, killing two and wounding four.[15] Afghan American Najibullah Zazi, who trained with Al Qaeda in Pakistan in 2008, came close to attacking the New York

City subway in September 2009, with a plan to place backpack bombs on crowded trains going to and from Grand Central and Times Square stations.[16] Faisal Shahzad, who trained with terrorists in the tribal regions of Pakistan, attempted but failed to detonate a crude car bomb in Times Square on May 1, 2010.[17] While all three were dangerous lone wolves, none fit the profile of would-be terrorists targeted today in FBI terrorism sting operations. Unlike those caught in FBI stings, these three terrorists had international connections and the ability to carry out attacks on their own, however unsuccessful those attacks might have been for Zazi and Shahzad.

By contrast, consider another New York City terrorism conspiracy—the so-called Herald Square bomb plot. Shahawar Matin Siraj, a twenty-two-year-old Pakistani American, struck up a friendship with a seemingly elderly and knowledgeable Islamic scholar named Dawadi at his uncle's Islamic books and tapes shop in Brooklyn. Dawadi was an FBI informant, Osama Eldawoody, who was put on the government payroll in September 2003 to stoke Siraj's extremist inclinations by claiming to have a degree in nuclear engineering, showing him pictures from Abu Ghraib, and bragging about his ties to "The Brotherhood," which Eldawoody said had connections to Omar Abdel-Rahman, the Egyptian commonly known as The Blind Sheikh who is serving a life sentence for his role in the 1993 World Trade Center bombings.[18] Siraj asked if Eldawoody could help him build a nuclear weapon and volunteered that he and a friend, James Elshafay, wanted to detonate a car bomb on one of New York's bridges. "He's a terrorist. He wants to harm the country and the people of the country. That's what I thought immediately," Eldawoody said in court testimony.

Siraj introduced Dawadi to Elshafay, who had drawn

schematics of police stations and bridges on napkins with the hopes of plotting a terrorist attack. Elshafay's crude drawings prompted Siraj to hatch a new plan that involved the three men, Dawadi's supposed international connections, and an attack on New York's Herald Square subway station. The two young men discussed how they'd grown to hate the United States for invading Iraq and torturing prisoners. In Eldawoody's car, the three of them talked about carrying twenty- to thirty-pound backpack bombs into the Herald Square subway station and leaving them on the train platform. Their conversations were recorded by a secret camera in the car's dashboard. From April to August 2004, the men considered targets, surveilled the subway, checked security, and drew diagrams of the station. The informant goaded them on the whole time, encouraging the pair with lines like: "We will teach these bastards a good lesson."[19] For his work on the case, Eldawoody received $100,000 from the FBI.

The evidence from the sting was enough to win convictions, and Siraj was sentenced to thirty years in prison and Elshafay to five years. But it was also clear from the trial that Siraj was a dimwitted social recluse—a mother's boy with little capacity to steal a car on his own, let alone bomb a subway station as part of a spectacular terrorist attack that could frighten the most populous city in the United States. In fact, Siraj was recorded during the sting operation as saying: "Everyone thinks I'm stupid." The question underlying the Herald Square case can be asked in dozens of other similar sting operations: Could the defendants have become terrorists had they never met the FBI informant? The answer haunts Martin Stolar, the lawyer who represented Siraj at trial and fully expected to win an acquittal through an entrapment defense. "The problem with the cases we're talking about is that defendants would not have done anything if not kicked in the ass by government agents," Stolar said. "They're creating crimes to solve crimes so they can claim a victory in the War on Terror."[20] The practice is only growing. Though developed under the watch of President George W. Bush, terrorism stings have become even more common under the Obama administration. While the Bush administration's use of terrorism stings peaked in 2006 and 2007—sixty defendants were prosecuted and convicted from terrorism stings during those two years—the Justice Department began to shy away from the practice toward the end of Bush's term in office. In 2008, Bush's last year as president, the U.S. government didn't prosecute anyone from a terrorism sting. But when Barack Obama became president in January 2009, the use of sting operations resumed and increased in frequency. During Obama's first three years in office, the Justice Department prosecuted more than seventy-five terrorism sting targets.[21]

More than anything, these aggressive prosecutions are a result of Obama's embracing national security as a central tenet of his presidency. Despite having been awarded a Nobel Peace Prize in 2009, Obama has been an agressive president—engaging U.S. military resources in the ouster of Muammar Gaddafi in Libya and conducting secret wars in Yemen and Somalia. But nowhere is Obama's agressiveness more dramatic than at home, where he has ordered six prosecutions under the 1917 Espionage Act involving leaks of government documents—double the number of Espionage Act prosecutions under all previous presidents combined—and stepped up the rate of terrorism sting operations conducted by the FBI.[22] Obama's national security posture is a pragmatic political one, as the public has historically perceived Democrats as weak on national security and unwilling to be as aggressive on terrorism as their Republican counterparts. However, Obama was able to reverse that perception during his first years in office, and public opinion polls during his fourth year as president showed that most Americans gave him high marks on national security.[23]

That's in part why the Obama administration has been so aggressive in pursuing terrorism stings. Addressing a gathering of Muslim leaders near San Francisco in December 2010, attorney general Eric Holder explained that in the use of terrorism stings, the administration believes the ends justify the means. "These types of operations have proven to be an essential law enforcement tool in uncovering and preventing potential terror attacks ... And in those terrorism cases where undercover sting operations have been used, there is a lengthy record of convictions," the Attorney General said, adding "Our nation's law enforcement professionals have consistently demonstrated not just their effectiveness, but also their commitment to the highest standards of professional conduct, integrity, and fairness."[24]

Today, federal prosecutors announce arrests from terrorism stings at a rate of about one every sixty days, suggesting either that there are a lot of ineffective terrorists in the United States, or that the FBI has become effective at creating the very enemy it is hunting.

2. THE NEW FBI

The story of the FBI's transformation from a law enforcement organization that investigates crimes after they occur to one that tries to prevent them before they happen began with an agent whose life ended in the south tower of the World Trade Center on September 11, 2001.

John P. O'Neill was a handsome man who wore his black hair slicked back and every morning placed a pocket square in his custom-tailored suit jacket. He had moved up in the Bureau after investigating white-collar crime and abortion clinic bombings, and had a reputation for being unafraid to challenge superiors, high-level political appointees, and politicians. He was what most FBI agents weren't—flamboyant and opinionated.

In 1995, following an assignment in Chicago, O'Neill received a promotion that brought him to FBI headquarters in Washington, D.C., where he was named chief of the counterterrorism section. Back then, counterterrorism was a small FBI branch that rarely attracted the notice of the Bureau's leadership. However, his first day on the job, O'Neill received a tip that would begin an obsession with a terrorist organization known as Al Qaeda. Ramzi Yousef, mastermind of the 1993 World Trade Center bombing and co-conspirator of the "Bojinka" bomb plot (a foiled 1995 attempt to hide explosives in dolls placed aboard airliners), had been spotted in Pakistan. O'Neill put together a team including Pakistan's Inter-Services Intelligence that captured Yousef in Islamabad and extradited him to New York, where he was found guilty at trial for his role in the World Trade Center bombing and sentenced to life in prison.

Following Yousef's capture, O'Neill began to suspect that Al Qaeda, then an emerging Islamic terrorist network, would try to target the United States again. Al Qaeda was more sophisticated and farther-reaching than U.S. government officials had estimated, O'Neill believed. However, his obsession with Al Qaeda and his abrasive personal style chafed at FBI headquarters. Following a heated exchange with then FBI director Louis Freeh on a plane trip from Saudi Arabia—O'Neill told the director Saudi officials were "blowing smoke up your ass" about the Khobar Towers bombing investigation—O'Neill put in for a transfer to the New York office.[1] When the Bureau granted his request, he moved the FBI's counterterrorism section to Manhattan and set out to recruit agents for a re-configured unit that would investigate an emerging enemy the FBI only barely understood.

Dedicating itself to researching Al Qaeda and Osama bin Laden, the counterterrorism section found evidence to support O'Neill's belief that Al Qaeda was getting Muslim extremists throughout the Middle East and Asia to coalesce around a common philosophy that viewed the United States as a central force for evil in the world. But the Bureau's top leaders weren't interested in what O'Neill was finding, and his warnings about Al Qaeda's increasing threat to the United States fell on deaf ears at headquarters. After being denied a promotion to head the FBI's New York office, one of the Bureau's most prestigious posts, O'Neill, then forty-nine years old, knew he'd reached the top rung of his ladder at the Bureau and submitted his retirement paperwork in August 2001.

O'Neill had lined up another job, however, as chief of security at the World Trade Center. He told Chris Isham about his new job. Isham was an ABC News producer who had interviewed Osama bin Laden in May 1998 and had leaned on O'Neill for information to prepare the interview questions. "Well, that'll be an easy job," Isham told him. "They're not going to bomb that place again."[2]

"No, actually, they've always wanted to finish that job," O'Neill told him. "I think they're going to try again."

Nineteen days after O'Neill started at the World Trade Center, two commercial airliners crashed into the twin towers. O'Neill died in the attack from an enemy he had repeatedly told the FBI it should fear. Despite his death and the resistance to his warnings about Al Qaeda, O'Neill's ideas and several agents he trained would ultimately reshape the Bureau's counterterrorism section in the years following the attack.

Because of the long-term institutional ignorance about the threat that Al Qaeda posed, most of the FBI's top management knew little about the terrorist organization on September 11, 2001. Part of the reason for this problem was that counterterrorism before 9/11 was considered a career dead end within the Bureau. As a result, FBI training did not distinguish between Islamic terror tactics and those that had been employed in the past by European and domestic groups. "A bombing case is a bombing case," said Dale Watson, who was the FBI's assistant director for counterterrorism on Sep-

tember 11, 2001.[3] During a 2004 deposition, a lawyer asked
the former counterterrorism chief if he knew the difference
between Shia and Sunni Muslims. "Not technically, no," he
answered. Watson's attitude reflected a belief in the Bureau
that agents didn't need to understand Al Qaeda in order to
investigate the terrorist network. "I don't necessarily think
you have to know everything about the Ku Klux Klan to investigate a church bombing," Watson said in the same deposition as a way of explaining this thinking.[4]

The Bureau's ignorance of Al Qaeda and Islamic terrorism in general was one of the reasons the FBI was
caught flatfooted on September 11, 2001. But it wasn't
the only reason. Despite his unsophisticated view of Islam, Watson had lobbied to increase the counterterrorism
budget. With the help of outside consultants, and with the
approval of President Bill Clinton's attorney general, Janet Reno, Watson had authored a plan codenamed MAX
CAP 05, or Maximum Capacity by 2005, which called
for a significant capacity increase in FBI counterterrorism operations. In the months before 9/11, as intelligence
suggested a terrorist attack could be imminent, Watson
pushed Attorney General John Ashcroft to approve MAX
CAP 05. But Ashcroft and Robert Mueller—then the attorney general's deputy at the Justice Department—rejected Watson's requests for budgetary reasons.[5] That left the
FBI counterterrorism section poorly equipped to respond
to the 9/11 attacks. As the U.S. government prepared for
a feared second-wave attack, few agents were qualified to
gather intelligence effectively and quickly on Islamic terrorism, in the United States or abroad. For example, on
the day planes flew into the World Trade Center, the FBI
had only eight agents who could speak Arabic and only

one of those agents, Ali Soufan, an O'Neill protégé, was based in New York.[6]*

FBI director Robert Mueller had taken the top job at the Bureau only one week before 9/11. After the World Trade Center towers fell, President George W. Bush called the new director into the Oval Office. He had a simple message for him: never again. The White House began to exert enormous pressure on the FBI to disrupt or preempt the feared next attack, forcing the Bureau to transform overnight into an intelligence-gathering agency capable of doing what international peer groups such as Britain's MI5 were able to achieve in terms of surveillance. To help accomplish this, the FBI recruited intelligence officers out of the National Security Agency and Central Intelligence Agency. Mueller's stewardship of the FBI's rapid transformation was among the reasons he received favorable reviews from the 9/11 Commission.[7]

To lead the transformation into a counterintelligence and counterterrorism organization, Mueller turned to Pat D'Amuro, who had researched Al Qaeda while working under John O'Neill. In D'Amuro, whose background was in investigating Russian organized crime, O'Neill had seen a talented manager who could help him run the counterterrorism

---

*This ignorance of Islam and Islamic culture pervades the Bureau's highest ranks to this day, as the FBI's few Muslim agents have had trouble climbing the ranks. In one of several examples of alleged discrimination, the FBI denied the promotion of one Muslim agent, Bassem Youssef, due in part to confusing him with another Muslim agent, Gamal Abdel-Hafiz, who was fired, but later reinstated, after refusing to wear a wire during the controversial investigation of Sami Al-Arian, a computer engineering professor at the University of South Florida in Tampa who pleaded guilty to conspiring to provide services to the Palestinian Islamic Jihad following years of FBI scrutiny.

section. "I can teach you the counterterrorism issues," O'Neill told D'Amuro.[8] Mueller knew that O'Neill's former unit in New York was the most up to speed on Al Qaeda, and that D'Amuro, as O'Neill's former deputy, was best qualified to lead an investigation of 9/11. "I was down in Washington and the director saw me in the hallway and wanted to speak to me," D'Amuro remembered. "So I went into his office the next day and that's when he asked me if I would come down to Washington as an inspector-in-place and run the events of 9/11 because of the involvement of New York into the investigations and the intelligence gathering into Al Qaeda."[9] That post led to D'Amuro's quick promotion to executive assistant director for counterintelligence and counterterrorism.

In an effort to redesign the FBI's counterterrorism program, D'Amuro called Arthur Cummings, a former Navy SEAL who spoke Mandarin and had investigated the first World Trade Center bombing, and asked him to take the position of counterterrorism section chief.[10] Because counterterrorism still had a reputation at the Bureau for being a career-halting transfer, Cummings, who was based in Richmond, Virginia, was initially resistant. He wanted to move up in the Bureau, and he knew some paths made upward movement easier than others. Counterterrorism wasn't one of those paths, Cummings and other FBI agents believed at the time. Cummings told D'Amuro he didn't want the job, as he had put in to be assistant special agent in charge, or ASAC, of the FBI's office in Richmond.

D'Amuro asked FBI director Mueller to call Cummings himself. "He said that he understood that I wanted to be the ASAC in Richmond, and I said I did," Cummings recalled. "I said that would be my preference because I needed to ensure my career progression, and the Bureau's a little tight on checking the boxes. I just needed to be an ASAC, or I thought I did. He said, 'It's a different time. You've already displayed leadership traits. You don't need to be an ASAC. Don't worry about being an ASAC. I need you in this section chief job.'"[11] D'Amuro added that Cummings was getting the terrorism post whether he wanted it or not. "He basically said, 'I need you in this job. It's very important right now in counterterrorism,'" Cummings said. "And I said, 'It doesn't make sense from a career progression standpoint. He said, 'You can either put in for the job or I'm going to draft you for the job. But you're going to do this job.' The Bureau, after 9/11, stopped being an all-volunteer army. The director made it very clear that he needed the right people in the right jobs at the right time. He basically was making that happen. So I said OK. I'm not an idiot. I was going to be in the job. I was either going to go willingly or I was going to not, but I was going to be in the job."[12] While Cummings was rebuilding the counterterrorism section in Washington, D.C., FBI associate deputy director Thomas J. Harrington sent him to Guantanamo Bay, Cuba, in January 2003 to help set up the FBI's operations on the island. Harrington saw it as an opportunity for Cummings and other counterterrorism agents and analysts to get "in the box" with terrorists and build their confidence in dealing one on one with Islamic extremists.[13] When he returned from Cuba, Cummings had orders to devise the Department of Homeland Security's new threat-level matrix—the now-famous red, orange, and blue color scheme.[14] "They started off with the red, orange, green," Cummings said. "I've got some great stories about that whole disaster. What are color-blind people going to do? I mean, the questions that came."[15]

Among Cummings's most important tasks at the Bureau

was increasing intelligence gathering at home. As a result, he became one of the chief proponents of FBI terrorism stings, co-authoring the Bureau's Domestic Investigations and Operations Guide, best known by the acronym DIOG. The 258-page document created the policy framework for the FBI's domestic intelligence network in U.S. Muslim communities and elsewhere, and allowed the Bureau to open quick investigations, known as "threat assessments," without having the criminal predicate, or probable cause, necessary to justify a full investigation.[16] Before 9/11, investigating anyone without having credible information to support the belief that the target was involved in a crime was illegal—and unthinkable at the FBI. The DIOG changed all of that, and specifically allowed the consideration of religious affiliation for justifying threat assessments. If a known or suspected terrorist had attended a particular mosque, for example, the FBI had authority under the DIOG to investigate any of the mosque's other attendees for up to forty-eight hours. Once forty-eight hours had passed, according to the DIOG, agents needed an established predicate to continue the investigation. The current version of the DIOG, adopted in October 2011, goes even further than the one Cummings co-wrote, allowing for, among other tactics, "trash covers," which is Bureau parlance for when agents rifle through someone's garbage to search for information that could be used to recruit informants.[17]

A well-built man with a strong jawline and light brown hair pulled back from a balding scalp, Cummings worked to change the culture of FBI investigations. Instead of arresting a would-be terrorist as soon as agents had sufficient evidence, as was the protocol before 9/11, FBI men and women under Cummings left targets in the wild longer to be monitored and tracked. This allowed agents to gather as much information as they could about possible terrorists and their associates.[18] Cummings pressed FBI agents to find not only the suspected terrorist but also the web of people linked to the suspected terrorist.

But increasingly what Cummings and his agents discovered was that the threats weren't coming from a network of people—the FBI, a few years after 9/11, had become less concerned about terrorist cells—but instead from young men acting alone. The threat had shifted from an organized group to a lone wolf, Cummings believed. With the intelligence apparatuses of several nations focused on Al Qaeda in Afghanistan and Pakistan, it had become nearly impossible for the organization to train a group of terrorists and then send them to the United States or Europe without being intercepted. Simply, a 9/11-style attack was no longer within Al Qaeda's capability. The best the organization could do was inspire someone already in the West to carry out a terrorist attack—an attack Al Qaeda's leadership would likely know nothing about until it happened—and then claim credit once the smoke had cleared. That's why the FBI became so obsessed with the possibility of a lone-wolf attack; the Bureau now believed that at any time, in any community, someone could radicalize and become a terrorist, with a bomb, a gun, even with household chemicals.

In light of this new theory, the main concern at the Bureau became how to identify these lone wolves *before* they struck. To assist with this, the FBI came up with a kind of radicalization spectrum, running from sympathizer to operator. All operators were sympathizers at one point, the spectrum theory goes, but not all sympathizers become operators. "We're looking for the sympathizer who wants to become an operator, and we want to catch them when they step over that line to operator," Cummings said. "Sometimes, that step takes ten years.

Other times, it takes ten minutes." The FBI tries to identify those who might take this step by scrutinizing Muslims who are espousing radical beliefs, expressing hatred of the United States or its foreign policy, or associating with others who are doing one of those two things. The FBI obtains some of this information through tips or by monitoring radical forums and chat rooms online. But the majority of this information comes from the street level, from informants.

Throughout the FBI's history, the numbers of informants the Bureau employs has been a closely guarded secret. Periodically, however, these figures have been made public. A Senate oversight committee in 1975 found the FBI had 1,500 informants. In 1980, officials disclosed there were 2,800. Six years later, following the FBI's push into drugs and organized crime, the number of informants ballooned to 6,000, according to the *Los Angeles Times*.[19] That number grew significantly after 9/11. For example, in its fiscal year 2008 budget authorization request, the FBI disclosed that it had been working under a secret November 2004 presidential directive demanding an increase in "human source development and management," and that it needed $12.7 million for a program to keep tabs on its spy network and create software to track and manage 15,000 informants.

The FBI's use of informants today is unprecedented. In addition to the roster of 15,000 informants that the Bureau maintains—many of them tasked with infiltrating Muslim communities in the United States—for every informant officially listed, there are as many as three unofficial ones, known in FBI parlance as "hip pockets." Informants can be doctors, clerks, imams. Some might not even consider themselves informants. But the FBI regularly taps all of them as part of a domestic intelligence apparatus whose only historical peer might be Cointelpro, the program the Bureau ran from the 1950s to the 1970s to discredit and marginalize groups ranging from the Ku Klux Klan to the Communist Party to the Reverend Martin Luther King Jr.'s civil rights organization.

To manage this comprehensive system, the FBI uses a computer program known as Delta, which allows agents to search the ranks of informants using specific parameters—among them age, ethnicity, nation of origin, and languages spoken. "The idea behind Delta was to make it more efficient not only to document information, but to manage information and incorporate elements of oversight," Wayne Murphy, the FBI's assistant director of intelligence, told the news media when Delta was first announced to the public in July 2007.[20] Effective informants today move around the country doing the FBI's bidding, and Delta has made this fluent movement possible. An FBI informant who can look and speak the terrorist part can move from case to case, jurisdiction to jurisdiction, state to state, earning tens of thousands of dollars at every stop. It's not uncommon for informants to make $100,000 or more on a case, plus a "performance incentive" of potentially tens of thousands of dollars if the case results in convictions, and then move across the country to do it all over again in some other city. Delta streamlines the horse-trading of informants among FBI handlers by cataloging them and providing detailed information about their case histories. Using Delta, FBI agents who need an informant can search the database and find candidates—just as a corporate recruiter might use LinkedIn while searching for software engineers to hire.

In addition to dramatically changing the way the FBI tracks and uses informants, Delta also put a stop to an older, rampant practice of agents hoarding the best informants for job security. Peter Ahearn, the retired FBI special agent who oversaw the Joint Terrorism Task Force in Western New York, explained to me how after Delta was implemented, agents could no longer guard their informants—in the past, agents had treated informants like their personal pets, to be let out of their cages only when necessary and never to be shared with other agents—because there was now a digital clearinghouse of snitches. If agents in a particular city needed an informant for a certain task, all they had to do was load Delta and see which informants might be available for transfer. "I could sit down in front of a computer and type in 'one-legged Somali,' and I'd find we've got one in Kansas City, and I could call up the handler and ask if I could borrow the guy," Ahearn told me, exaggerating for humor.[21]

The FBI's extensive and better-organized use of informants represents one great change for the Bureau in the post–9/11 era. But another—and perhaps more jarring—change involves data mining. Before 9/11, due to security concerns and an antiquated computer system, most FBI agents couldn't even search the Internet from their desks, let alone track terrorists. In fact, on September 11, 2001, FBI agents were forced to send photographs of the hijackers by express mail because the Bureau's computer system didn't allow them to email images. Former FBI director Louis Freeh, who retired in June 2001, was so technology averse that he refused to use email. U.S. Senator Charles E. Schumer has described the Bureau's outdated computer system and Luddite culture as the FBI's "greatest failure" under Freeh.[22]

That the FBI was behind the times technologically is an understatement, and so using data for intelligence purposes represented a giant leap forward for the Bureau. To assist in taking that leap, in 2005, FBI director Mueller tapped Philip Mudd, a former CIA analyst and top-level briefer under CIA director George Tennant. Mudd had risen to second-in-command of the CIA Counterterrorism Center, which oversees all clandestine operations involving Al Qaeda and other terrorist groups. Mudd's move to the FBI was a very unusual one for a CIA man. While interagency cooperation has increased significantly since 9/11, strong rivalries and prejudices still exist among federal law enforcement agencies. The CIA, FBI, DEA, Bureau of Alcohol, Tobacco, Firearms and Explosives (ATF)—each is suspicious of the other. The FBI views the CIA as a group of bluebloods whose job is made easy by not being bound by the U.S. Constitution. The CIA, in turn, views the FBI as a ragtag group of desk-jockeying accountants and lawyers who hate to get their hands dirty with fieldwork. The CIA and FBI view DEA and ATF agents as underachievers, and, in turn, DEA and ATF agents believe the CIA and FBI are filled with ineffectual snobs. In short, the agencies don't trust each other, and any agent switching teams is received with intense suspicion. "There's always been this competition and distrust," Dale Watson, the FBI's former assistant director for counterterrorism, who did a detail assignment at the CIA in the mid-1990s, told me. "No one at the FBI trusted the CIA enough to share a lot of information, and vice versa."[23] Because of this mistrust, there were significant misgivings about Mudd when he arrived as deputy director of the FBI's new National Security Branch, whose creation President George W. Bush ordered in 2005 to consolidate the Bureau's counterterrorism, counterintelligence, and intelligence capabilities under one department. Among seasoned FBI agents, there was a belief that Mudd would try to remake the Bureau into a domestic CIA. In many ways this has come true, as Mudd has altered the way the Bureau operates, pushing agents to increase their intelligence-gathering capability, in particular by increasing the number of informants they have on the streets providing them with information.

To coordinate intelligence gathering and informant recruitment, Mudd took over a program called Domain Management, which the FBI had created to track immigrants from China and other countries who were suspected of being involved in industrial espionage—mainly the theft of intellectual property from corporations and universities. Mudd expanded Domain Management to use commercially available data, as well as government data from I-9 "Employment Eligibility Verification" immigration forms, to pinpoint the demographics of specific ethnic and religious communities— say, for example, Iraqis in central Los Angeles or Pakistanis in the Washington, D.C., suburbs.* In February 2006, shortly after taking his position at the FBI, Mudd demonstrated Domain Management to high-ranking agents. He displayed a map of the San Francisco Bay area, which highlighted the places where Iranian immigrants were living. That was where, Mudd said, the FBI was "hunting." [24] Domain Management could tell FBI agents with precision where Muslims lived in San Francisco—as well as nationwide—allowing them to direct resources and informant recruitment to specific neighborhoods.

---

*The commercial data that the FBI feeds into Domain Management has been a matter of some debate. *Congressional Quarterly* reported that consumer data used in Domain Management once included grocery store sales of Middle Eastern food. The FBI denied that it was data mining falafel transactions, calling the report "too ridiculous to be true," but *Congressional Quarterly* stood by its story.

The FBI officially denies that Domain Management works this way. Its purpose, Bureau spokespeople have said, is simply to help allocate resources according to threats. But FBI agents have told me that with counterterrorism as the Bureau's top priority, agents often look for those threats in Muslim communities—and Domain Management allows agents to understand those communities' locations and demographics. One former FBI official jokingly referred to Domain Management as "Battlefield Management."

Some FBI veterans have criticized Domain Management as unproductive and intrusive—one agent told Mudd during a high-level meeting that the program pushed the Bureau to "the dark side." This tension has its roots in the stark difference between the FBI and the CIA. While the latter is free to operate internationally without regard to constitutional rights, the FBI must respect those rights in domestic investigations. Mudd's critics inside the Bureau saw the targeting of Americans based on their ethnicity and religion as going a step too far. For his part, Mudd brushed off the criticism as coming from old-school agents unwilling to adapt to a rapidly changing world. "There's 31,000 employees in this organization and we're undergoing a sea-change," he told the *New York Times* during his first year at the FBI. "It's going to take a while for what is a high-end national security program to sink down to every officer."[25]

But internal FBI documents obtained by the American Civil Liberties Union in December 2011 suggest that Mudd's critics had reason to be concerned. The documents show that since 2005, the FBI has used its community outreach programs—which had previously been operated out of the FBI's Office of Public Affairs—to gather intelligence on people not suspected of having committed crimes. In other words, no criminal predicate existed to justify an investigation. Many of the activities documented through this intelligence gathering were religious ones protected by the First Amendment, such as where and when Muslims worshipped. The FBI then fed the information collected into Domain Management for future analysis. In a March 2008 memorandum, for example, FBI agents wrote about an outreach effort to a Pakistani American community organization in San Francisco.[26] In the memorandum, the FBI agents documented religious activity and the identities of the organization's officers and directors. The year before, in 2007, agents were present at a mosque outreach meeting in San Jose, California, that was attended by fifty people representing twenty-seven local Muslim communities. A resulting FBI memorandum, which was included in three case files, identified each of the fifty participants by name and affiliation and then analyzed the demographics of the attendees.[27]

Historically, the FBI's community outreach programs were designed to build trust between federal law enforcement and local communities—to make it easier for the FBI to investigate crimes by having a public more willing to volunteer tips and information. But under Domain Management, community outreach programs now serve as Trojan horses for intelligence-gathering agents, giving them cover as they harvest information under the guise of community engagement. The FBI then uses this information to determine where to assign informants and agents and what screws to turn when trying to win cooperation from would-be informants in Muslim communities. Some FBI agents under Domain Management are assigned full-time to recruiting informants, and these agents often use immigration violations, evidence of crimes, and embarrassing information, such as about extramarital relationships, to coerce Muslims into becoming informants, who in turn tell the FBI under duress about other Muslims they should consider targeting for scrutiny.

It was a cloudy winter's day in February 2011 when I arrived at the FBI Academy in Quantico, Virginia, a sandstone fortress of a building on a 385-acre Marine Corps base west of Interstate 95. I had asked J. Stephen Tidwell to help me understand how and why the FBI employs Domain Management and its thousands of informants. Now executive director of FBI National Academy Associates, a nonprofit that organizes training sessions at the FBI Academy for local law enforcement, Tidwell retired in 2010 as an executive assistant director of the FBI. While at Bureau headquarters, he authored the Domestic Investigations and Operations Guide with Arthur Cummings, and before that oversaw a large and controversial intelligence-gathering operation that recruited informants from and spied on members of Muslim communities in Southern California.

Tidwell arguably knows as much about FBI counterterrorism operations as anyone, and on that February afternoon, he drove me in his black Ford F350 through Hogan's Alley, a ten-acre recreation of a town at the FBI Academy crowded with houses, bars, stores, and a hotel, which the Bureau uses as "a realistic training ground" for its new agents.[28] The FBI jokingly refers to Hogan's Alley—which gets its name from a nineteenth-century comic strip—as "a hotbed of terrorist and criminal activity," and agents who work sting operations learn their craft here. At one end of the town is the Biograph Theater, named for the Chicago movie house where FBI agents gunned down John Dillinger in 1934. Tidwell pointed to the model cinema and laughed. "Dillinger, Biograph Theater, Chicago," he said. "See, the FBI has a sense of humor."

A former West Texas cop, Tidwell is a barrel-chested man with close-cropped brown hair that is slowly graying. Wearing khakis, a blue sweater, and an oxford shirt, he drove me back to the main FBI Academy building and continued the nickel tour. In one of the hallways, he stopped at and pointed to a plaque hanging on the wall, which commemorated John O'Neill. "John understood the threat Al Qaeda posed long before anyone else at the Bureau did," Tidwell said. We then walked to the office of FBI National Academy Associates, which is tucked into a corner of the FBI Academy's main building. Not far from Tidwell's neatly kept, windowed office is a place where visitors can buy FBI Academy souvenirs such as T-shirts and coffee mugs.

Many current and former FBI agents I've spoken to have offered negative comments about Domain Management and its creator, Philip Mudd, drawing a caricature of the former CIA analyst as a soulless purveyor of the dark arts whose evils have infected the Bureau. Tidwell isn't one of them. In fact, he's one of Mudd's most vocal supporters. I asked him whether he believed Domain Management's obvious intrusion into minority communities, with maps created according to demographic and religious data, was worth whatever benefits could be achieved for criminal investigations and intelligence gathering. Tidwell leaned back in his chair and crossed his legs, placing his left foot on top of his right knee, as he thought about how to answer the question. "I don't think it's useful to think of Domain Management strictly in the way you are," he told me. "Let's imagine we're out in a field to investigate a report that there's been a murder. We're looking for the body, and it's all woods and brush except for a large barn in the middle of the property. One person suggests that we divide up the property into sections and have agents walk it inch by inch until we find the body. Another suggests that we get up on the roof of the barn and look for the body from that vantage point. But a third person says neither of those plans is the most effective way to find the body. He instead points to the sky, where birds are circling. He says, 'Let's search the ground those birds are flying over.' That's what Domain Management does."

However, there's a significant difference between Tidwell's analogy and Domain Management. In Tidwell's analogy, the birds provide an independent third-party analysis of sorts—their presence in the sky suggests that a body could be below, no matter what preconceived ideas FBI agents might have about the location of the reported murder victim. But with Domain Management, the data provides suggestions that bolster, rather than challenge, the FBI's preconceived ideas. The program is able to say with certainty and exactness where Muslims live in a particular city, but the belief that a danger exists in that part of the city as a result of the Muslim population requires the preconceived belief that Muslim communities represent a threat to public safety and national security. This belief and a generalized Islamophobia pervade all levels of the Bureau. In recent years, FBI counterterrorism training has made little to no distinction between the Al Qaeda terrorist network—whose members are religious radicals—and Islam in general. FBI counterterrorism training documents in circulation in 2011 described Mohammed as a "cult leader" and labeled charity among Muslims as a "funding mechanism for combat." The more devout a Muslim was, according to FBI training literature first made public by *Wired* magazine, the more likely he was to be violent.[29]

Tidwell understands better than most at the FBI the repercussions of focusing investigative resources on Muslims—he is a named defendant in a class-action lawsuit filed by the ACLU and Council on American-Islamic Relations in 2011 alleging illegal spying on Muslim communities in California—but he doesn't believe that knowing, for example, where Lebanese live in a city means that the FBI is necessarily spying on or targeting Lebanese Americans.[30] "Anything we do is going to be interpreted as monitoring Muslims," Tidwell said. "I would tell Muslim community leaders, 'Do you really think I have the time and money to monitor all the mosques and Arab American organizations? We don't, and I don't want to. The flip side with what the Bureau does is that we're also responsible nationally for protecting civil rights. That's something I always said in dealing with the Muslim communities—my first responsibility is to protect you. If a mosque had stuff painted on it, just like with a synagogue, we'd help clean it up. Our first responsibility to you is civil rights. Our second responsibility is making sure someone isn't hiding among you, taking advantage of what you represent."

Yet that second responsibility is the reason the FBI developed Domain Management, has agents who are assigned full-time to recruiting informants, and now needs sophisticated software to track its thousands of informants nationwide. The use of Domain Management and the explosive growth of the FBI informant ranks are the primary reasons why today we have so many terrorism sting cases. While the cases involve plots that sound dangerous—about bombing skyscrapers and synagogues and crowded public squares—if you dig deeper, you see that many of the government's alleged terrorists seem hopeless; they are almost always young and down on their luck, penniless, without much promise in their lives, easily susceptible to a strong-willed informant's influence. They're often blustery punks, I told Tidwell, and I wondered if most would mature past their big-talking ways if left alone. "And if they don't mature?" Tidwell countered. "Or if they hook up with someone of a like mind that has the capacity? You and I could sit here, go online, and by tonight have a decent bomb built. What do you do? Wait for him to figure it out himself?"

The FBI uses informants and terrorism stings to create a hostile environment for terrorist recruiters and operators—by raising the risk of even the smallest step toward violent action. It's a form of deterrence, an adaptation of the "broken windows" theory used to fight urban crime. Advocates such as Tidwell insist it has been effective, noting that there hasn't been a successful large-scale attack against the United States since 9/11. But what can't be answered—as many former and current FBI agents acknowledge—is how many of the Bureau's targets would have taken the step over the line at all were it not for the pressure and coercion of an informant.

3.MOHAMMED AND HOWARD

Informants have always been an integral part of the FBI, providing the eyes and ears on everything from the Prohibition-era Mafia, when informants furnished information about organized crime figures such as Al Capone, to the civil rights movement, when the FBI used, among other informants, African American freelance photographer Ernest Withers to infiltrate the organization of Dr. Martin Luther King Jr.[1] Under longtime director J. Edgar Hoover, however, informants never played an active role in FBI investigations; instead, they just watched and listened, and then reported what they saw and heard to their handlers at the Bureau.

This fly-on-the-wall approach metamorphosed during the war on drugs in the 1980s, when the FBI adopted a street-level approach to fighting crime. As part of this new approach, informants became active players in investigations, often posing as either drug dealers or buyers and saying and doing things that pushed plots forward or drew in additional targets. The terrorism informants of today are evolved versions of those drug war–era agents provocateurs.

The very first of this new breed of informant sprung up in Miami just before 9/11, putting together the kind of sting that would be replicated dozens of times over the next decade:

A target was identified—a disgruntled young Muslim man who said he wanted to launch an attack—and the informant then provided the means and opportunity for the attack, all the while secretly recording the target with hidden audio and video equipment. You might expect the informant who adapted the drug war–era "no-dope bust" for a new time and a new threat to be a grizzled, well-trained spy with a history of infiltrating dangerous, insular criminal organizations and bringing down high-profile crooks. But that wasn't the case at all. Instead, the man who deserves the credit for the change in FBI informant tactics was an inept, underachieving security guard who dreamed of a bullet-dodging, enemy-killing career as a spook with the Central Intelligence Agency.

The chief problem for Howard Gilbert—an overweight, middle-aged, Canadian-born Jewish man who had attended high school in Hollywood, Florida, and worked odd security jobs as an adult—was that he wasn't much like the bluebloods of the CIA. A Florida newspaper in 2002 described him as "a 340-pound man with a fondness for firearms and strippers."[2] When he wasn't working as a bodyguard or assassinating evil Latin American despots vicariously through *Soldier of Fortune* magazine, Gilbert could be found hanging around International Protective Services, a police and personal security store near downtown Hollywood, a few blocks from the train tracks Henry Flagler built from St. Augustine to Key West. International Protective Services garnered national attention after 9/11 for offering personal defense courses to American Airlines flight attendants—the wonderful irony being that terrorist ringleader Mohamed Atta had partied at Shuckum's Raw Bar & Grill, just a stone's throw from the doors of International Protective Services, before the deadly terrorist attack.

Gilbert had wanted in on the counterterrorism game before 9/11, as he saw it as a way of proving he was CIA material. In 2000, after attending the wedding of a Muslim friend, Gilbert hatched a plan to infiltrate the Darul Uloom mosque in the Miami suburb of Pembroke Pines. His idea was to pose as a Muslim convert named Saif Allah, meaning "sword of God" in Arabic. As one female congregant who asked not to be identified told me, everyone at the mosque was at first excited about Saif's arrival. "We were thrilled," she remembered. "The reaction was: 'Yeah! We got a white guy!'" Gilbert told everyone he was a disgruntled ex-Marine who was now working as a security expert, but some of the congregants at the mosque began to grow wary of the newest worshipper when Gilbert gave an inflammatory speech in late 2000 chiding Israel for what he described as its mistreatment of Palestinians and its refusal to adhere to previously drawn borders in allowing Israeli settlements in the West Bank. "That was truly the night that launched me into the terrorist umbrella of South Florida," Gilbert would later brag.

While the speech made many of the congregants suspicious, even frightened, of Gilbert, Imran Mandhai, a nineteen-year-old Broward Community College student, became enamored with him. Stirred by the oration, Mandhai approached Gilbert and asked if Gilbert could provide him with weapons and training. Since Gilbert had previously provided information to the FBI, primarily related to cases involving cargo theft, he already had contacts at the Bureau. He called his handlers at the North Miami Beach office and told them he wanted the assignment—and the paycheck—to work Mandhai as part of a counterterrorism case. The FBI agreed to put Gilbert on the books as an informant to see what might happen.

Mandhai told the newly minted FBI terrorism informant that he was angry with the U.S. government for having indicted his friend, a Turk named Hakki Cemal Aksoy, for immigration violations. While searching Aksoy's apartment, federal authorities had discovered bomb-making manuals; it's never been clear from available evidence whether Aksoy was on his way to becoming a terrorist or was just another immature young man fascinated with bombs and explosives. Gilbert told Mandhai he could help him take revenge against the government for indicting Aksoy, and he sold the young man a copy of *The Anarchist's Cookbook* for twenty dollars. Mandhai and a friend, Shueyb Mosaa Jokhan, then told Gilbert they wanted to bomb electrical transformers and a National Guard armory in South Florida as part of their quest for revenge. However, to build a terrorism conspiracy case, prosecutors needed more than just angry words about aspirational attacks: they needed the targets to do something—buy guns or bomb-making materials, take pictures of possible locations, transfer money. But because Gilbert was overeager, and a little awkward in the role of a terrorist, Mandhai began to suspect that Gilbert was an FBI mole, and he quickly closed up, putting the entire operation at risk.

In an attempt to keep the sting alive, the Bureau brought in another informant, Elie Assaad, an experienced snitch originally from Lebanon. How exactly Assaad came to work for the FBI is unclear. The story he tells seems incredulous, but it goes something like this: While he was living in Lebanon, a group of alleged terrorists asked him to bring a vial of some undetermined but reportedly dangerous substance into the United States. Assaad informed U.S. government officials of this while he was still in Lebanon, and they instructed him to board an airplane as planned and travel to Chicago with the substance, where he'd meet with FBI agents and hand over the vial. If the vial did in fact contain something dangerous, the obvious question that follows is why would U.S. government officials instruct Assaad to board a plane with it? Nevertheless, Assaad claimed that he traveled to Chicago, provided the vial to government agents, and that the FBI then put him on their payroll, sending him back to Lebanon as an informant. While he was in Lebanon, a car Assaad was riding in exploded—a bombing purportedly committed by the terrorist group who had provided the mysterious vial—and Assaad was badly burned in the blast. For his safety, FBI agents supposedly spirited him away to the United States, where he worked criminal and drug cases in Chicago for several years.

While working in the Windy City, however, Assaad failed an FBI lie detector test—which, under Bureau policy, should have disqualified him from future operations.[3] Informants who fail lie detector tests are disqualified for the obvious reason that they can no longer be trusted not to lie to their FBI handlers. The main difficulty in dealing with informants is that honest people don't make good ones. On the contrary, the best informants are professional liars who are able to develop personal relationships and then exploit those relationships, without remorse, for personal gain. U.S. Appeals Court Judge Stephen S. Trott, a Reagan appointee who was on the short list to be nominated as FBI director in 1987, is one of the nation's leading experts on criminal informants.[4] His 1996 law review article, "Words of Warning for Prosecutors Using Criminals as Witnesses," has become standard reading for criminal law students. Trott believes that the best informants are "sociopaths" whose negative social skills are necessary for effective criminal investigations. "They're sociopaths and one of the best things they can do is to lie. They're good at that,"

Trott told me.[5] "The Sisters of the Poor, the Delta Sorority, they're not going to help you catch bad guys. You just can't walk up to them and say, 'Hey, what's happening here?' You need your own bad guys to help you get subpoenas. You need your own bad guys to get information and help you build cases against other bad guys."

But that creates a challenge for the FBI: How can agents task an informant with lying to others and then be certain the informant isn't lying to them? Polygraph examinations, used when FBI agents debrief informants, provide the best solution for this dilemma—which is why as a policy the FBI disqualifies informants who are believed to have lied during a polygraph. However, Elie Assaad, having been caught lying to the FBI, kept on working for federal law enforcement. To this day, the Bureau has refused to release any information about the failed polygraph, other than the vague acknowledgment that agents caught Assaad lying. FBI officials have also declined on several opportunities to give me an explanation for why Assaad was not cut from the informant ranks. The only possible explanation for this is that Assaad got results as an informant, and that those results were impressive enough for the FBI to make an exception and keep him as an informant.

In early March 2001, trying to salvage Gilbert's ambitious but badly listing sting operation, Assaad introduced himself to Mandhai as "Mohammed." Gilbert made the introduction, and remained on the periphery as Assaad took charge of the operation. He was a terrorist with ties to Osama bin Laden, Assaad told the nineteen-year-old Mandhai, and his job was to establish a local training center for jihadists in Florida. Thinking he'd found his connection to Al Qaeda, Mandhai explained to Mohammed how he wanted to attack the power stations and National Guard armory and then contact the U.S. government to demand it stop supporting Israel. Assaad agreed to provide financial assistance. Mandhai also confided in Assaad that he suspected Howard Gilbert might be an FBI informant.

On March 13, Mandhai happened to mention an actual terrorist to Assaad—only Assaad and the U.S. government hadn't heard of him at the time. "Brother," Mandhai said, "why don't you come with us to Adnan … Probably he will join with us."[6] Adnan was Adnan Gulshair El Shukrijumah, who attended the same Florida community college as Mandhai and scratched out a living as a freelance computer technician. Shukrijumah lived in the suburban town of Miramar, where his father was an imam. Just before 9/11, he left the country and has never returned. The FBI now believes he is among Al Qaeda's top officials, and the U.S. government is offering $5 million for information leading to his capture. But back in 2001, when the federal government first became aware of him, Shukrijumah had no interest in joining Mandhai's amateurish plot to attack power stations and the armory. (He also reportedly turned down offers to become an FBI informant himself.)[7] In addition, Shukrijumah's brother thought it comical that the FBI considered Mandhai a potential terrorist. In an interview with the *Washington Post*, Nabil Shukrijumah said of Mandhai, "He's a naive … childish, very childish," adding that, "It's very funny to me that he was supposed to be recruiting people."[8]

Three days after mentioning Shukrijumah, and after having confessed to "Mohammed" that he believed Howard Gilbert was an FBI informant, Mandhai changed his story. He now told the FBI informants that he wasn't the leader of the bomb plot, and was in charge only of recruiting and operations for an idea and plan that had originated with Gilbert. The next day, Mandhai told Assaad and Gilbert that he was unwilling to move forward in the bomb plot. The FBI quickly severed Gilbert from the investigation, paying him $6,000 for his undercover work, since it appeared that Mandhai couldn't get past his suspicion that Gilbert was a snitch for the feds.

But Mandhai's mistrust of "Mohammed" didn't last. Once the FBI cut Gilbert from the sting, Mandhai contacted Assaad and asked for help in freeing Aksoy—the friend indicted for immigration violations. Aksoy could help with the bomb plot, Mandhai told Assaad, and he'd recruit twenty-five to thirty people to be trained at the Al Qaeda training camp. Assaad in turn presented Mandhai with an assortment of weapons and explosives as examples of what he could provide. Assaad, Mandhai, and his friend Shueyb Mosaa Jokhan then moved forward in the plot, first attending a gun show where they tried—but failed—to buy a gun. (Jokhan's credit card was declined.)

However, the whole operation came to a halt on April 6, 2001 when Miami-Dade police arrested Assaad at his apartment after his pregnant girlfriend called 911. When officers arrived, Maria Granados told them Assaad had beaten and choked her, and she had called authorities when she became fearful for the safety of her unborn child.[9] During questioning, Assaad told the police that he was unemployed. Granados ultimately spared Assaad by having prosecutors drop the felony aggravated battery charges against him.

One month after Assaad's arrest, FBI agents interviewed Imran Mandhai, and he admitted that he was planning to blow up electrical transformers and demand changes to U.S. foreign policy. One year later, after 9/11, federal prosecutors finally indicted Mandhai on two charges—conspiring to damage and destroy electrical power stations and a National Guard armory by means of fire and explosives, and inducing Jokhan to damage the property of an energy facility. Mandhai pleaded guilty to the first charge and received a sentence of 140 months. He is scheduled to be released in December 2014. Mandhai was the nation's first successful terrorism-related prosecution after September 11, 2001.[10]

While Howard Gilbert deserves credit for pioneering the aggressive terrorism sting operations in the Mandhai case that the FBI would replicate over the next decade, you won't hear his name in Congressional testimony or in laudations from FBI executives, because he never got public credit for his ideas. As a matter of fact, his life went into a tailspin shortly after Mandhai's arrest. He was officially outed as an informant in June 2002 when an FBI agent said his name during a pretrial hearing for Mandhai and the South Florida *Sun-Sentinel* reported the news on its front page. At the time, Gilbert was working as a limousine driver in Miami. Upon seeing his name in the newspaper, he did what you wouldn't expect from an aspiring CIA agent—he freaked out. Gilbert bought a second handgun and began hiding in hotel rooms, fearful that terrorists would try to assassinate him. Keith Ringel, a friend from Rhode Island, flew to Florida, and together he and Gilbert drove to Providence, traveling straight through and stopping only for gas. When Gilbert arrived at his friend's apartment, he placed the two handguns in a safe. But two days after their arrival, Ringel told Gilbert he had to get the guns out of the safe—he was having a party that evening and some of the attendees knew the safe's combination. Gilbert collected the guns and, using a holster, placed one of the guns on his hip. As Gilbert walked to his SUV, the gun visibly at his side, one of Ringel's neighbors called the cops to report an armed man in the apartment complex. Providence police arrived, and after admitting to officers that he did not have permits for the guns, Gilbert was arrested. State prosecutors charged him with two counts of carrying a pistol without a license—punishable by up to ten years in prison.

Broke and living out of his SUV in the parking lot of a Marriott Hotel, Gilbert was assigned public defenders Michael A. DiLauro and Anthony Capraro to help him fight the charges. Their defense was that Gilbert was under duress because he believed his life was in danger after being exposed as an FBI terrorism informant. DiLauro and Capraro subpoenaed records from the FBI—which failed to respond to the subpoenas. The Bureau's stonewalling proved as much of a problem for the prosecution as it did for the defense. Without FBI cooperation, the prosecution couldn't prove Gilbert *wasn't* in danger—that he was overreacting. James Dube, the prosecutor in the case, wanted desperately to bring in FBI agents from Florida to undermine Gilbert's claims of duress, and asked Superior Court Judge William A. Dimitri Jr. for more time, saying state officials needed to process the requests to allow Special Agents Keith Winter and Kevin O'Rourke to travel to Rhode Island.

"Don't give me that story," Dimitri told Dube. "Am I supposed to hold this trial until they're ready?"

"I can't be held accountable for what I don't have and a federal agency might have in its possession," Dube said.

"I do not dance to the tune of the FBI or the U.S. attorney in Florida," Dimitri said. "The FBI has been uncooperative since day one in this case." [11]

The prosecutor sent a transcript of that conversation to

the FBI in Miami, and on the day before the trial was to end, Winter and O'Rourke, as well as their boss, Supervisory Special Agent Mark Hastbacka, arrived in Providence to serve as rebuttal witnesses—to explain that Gilbert had never been in danger because the Mandhai prosecution didn't involve any actual terrorists. But given their late arrival, Judge Dimitri would not allow them to testify and dismissed the charges against Gilbert. The informant hugged his lawyers and promised to name his children after them, declaring them, with a nod to the O.J. Simpson murder trial, "better than any million-dollar dream team."[12]

But Gilbert would never have any children. In the winter of 2003, he returned to South Florida, working as bodyguard and a limousine driver and hanging around International Protective Services, just as he had before he became a terrorism informant. He was in a rut, and certainly not on a road leading to a future with the CIA, as he had once dreamed. In 2004, Gilbert was found dead. He had killed himself in the middle of the night, a silencer-equipped handgun to the head. Gilbert would never see how the FBI ultimately adopted the terrorism sting techniques he had developed in the Mandhai investigation, and how Elie Assaad, his fellow informant in that case, became a star snitch by refining those tactics in the case of the Liberty City Seven.

I was living in Miami on June 22, 2006, when the NBC affiliate interrupted regular television programming for a breaking news story. "We have some video that is just arriving from the scene," reporter Patricia Andreu told viewers. The video showed federal law enforcement officers wearing green uniforms and black boots as they walked in front of a ramshackle warehouse. "We're told that a terrorism-related investigation is under way," Andreu continued. "We're told that armed federal and local officials—there you see them right there— have set up a perimeter in the area. ... As you can see in this video that we just got into the NBC6 newsroom, several federal and local officials are on scene there, including the FBI. They're armed, as you can tell." The CBS affiliate quickly followed suit, posting a video on its website whose headline read, "Terror Suspects Detained by Agents in Projects."

That afternoon, federal agents had arrested seven alleged Al Qaeda operatives—Narseal Batiste, Patrick Abraham, Stanley Phanor, Naudimar Herrera, Burson Augustin, Lyglenson Lemorin, and Rotschild Augustine—who had supposedly plotted to blow up the Sears Tower in Chicago and the North Miami Beach office of the FBI. Though the media in Florida and around the country quickly portrayed the seven men as dangerous terrorists, immediate questions arose among people familiar with terrorism cases as to whether the charges were trumped up. "I firmly believe there are public relations aspects to this case and other cases like it," Khurrum Wahid, a Miami lawyer who has represented accused terrorists, told me the day after the arrests were announced. "It's clear to me that the federal government used this case to try and send a message about the threat of terrorism in Miami and the rest of the country."

The timing of the raid was suspicious as well, as the *New York Times* had just revealed on its website a secret Bush administration program that permitted, under the guise of counterterrorism, the CIA and the Treasury Department to review, without warrants or subpoenas, the financial transactions of U.S. citizens and others living in the United States— yet another program that raised questions about whether the Bush administration was overstepping its legal authority in the hunt for terrorists after 9/11.[13] The *Times* story had been in the works for months, and the Bush administration knew it was coming, so the announcement of a terrorist cell bust in Florida pushed that important story below the fold in most major newspapers the following day.

Max Rameau, a Haitian-born activist who led a project to monitor local police and another to seize vacant lots in Miami and build a shantytown for the homeless, and who knew personally the men the federal government charged as terrorists in the Liberty City case, believed that the arrests were specifically timed to coincide with the story in the *New York Times*. "I think the government's immediate intention in announcing the Liberty City Seven case was to draw attention away from the *New York Times* story coming out the next day," Rameau told me at his office on Northwest Fifteenth Avenue, in the heart of Liberty City, when I met with him in 2009. "The arrests happened on a Thursday. That Friday was the long-awaited *New York Times* story about how the Bush administration was spying on people's ATM transactions. But the day that story came out, it was downplayed because what became big news was the fact that these seven terrorists, black terrorists, reportedly Muslim terrorists, were arrested. I think the initial intention of it was to divert attention away from this story related to terrorism that was very damaging to the Bush administration and they wanted to trump that by showing there was some terrorism actually happening. Of course, they couldn't find any terrorism happening, so they had to manufacture this instead."[14]

Finally, the area of Miami where the alleged terrorists were arrested—Liberty City—seemed like a peculiar place for them to hide. The poorest section of Miami, Liberty City— which gets its name from the Liberty Square public housing project built in the mid-1930s under the New Deal—is a largely African American and Haitian American neighborhood that Miami's leaders would just as soon pretend didn't exist. The police presence in Liberty City is obvious at all hours of the day and night, and a number of nonprofit community organizations have feet on the ground there. In short, it's not a neighborhood where anyone—terrorists in particular—would likely go unnoticed.

None of this skepticism, however, was evident in the news media's initial coverage of the arrests. In one report, Rad Berky, a journalist for the Miami ABC affiliate, stood outside the group's warehouse in Liberty City as the phrases "Terror Raid" and "Terror Arrests" flashed across the screen. Berky reported the government's allegations in full, telling viewers that the seven men were preparing to launch attacks in Miami and Chicago. "There is also said to be audio- or videotape of the group members pledging support for violent holy war," he said. Berky's unquestioning, overhyped reporting of the government's claims is emblematic of the lapdog approach the media has taken in covering federal terrorism cases since September 11, 2001.

The main reason for this is cultural. After 9/11, there was a nearly unanimous belief at the FBI that terrorists were hiding in the United States, preparing to launch a second wave of attacks. Every current and former FBI agent I interviewed in researching this book told me they were certain that terrorist cells were embedded in the United States after September 11, 2001, and that the World Trade Center and Pentagon attacks were just the beginning. "We were bracing for the next attack," Dale Watson, the FBI's assistant director for counterterrorism on 9/11, told me. This was a popular belief nationwide in the first few years after 9/11; the Showtime television series *Sleeper Cell*, about a Muslim FBI agent who infiltrates a terrorist cell in Los Angeles, exemplified this national assumption that deadly terrorists were out there and we needed to find them before time ran out and innocent people were killed. The government's story of seven guys plotting to blow up a skyscraper and an FBI office fit perfectly with this widespread public assumption. If the media and the public believe terrorists are out there, they aren't likely to question the government about whether the men trotted out for the cameras are actual terrorists.

This attitude, which is still prevalent today, provides the government with a public suspension of disbelief whenever officials announce terrorism-related arrests. During the first few days of any crime story, even those unrelated to terrorism, law enforcement has a unique ability to control the narrative. Whenever local, state, or federal police announce a high-profile indictment, they do so with the luxury of operating in an information vacuum, as most, if not all, of the initial information comes from the police or prosecutors—details of the crimes and the defendants' backgrounds and motivations. It can take weeks, even months, before journalists are able to interview people related to the defendants or uncover information that provides a more nuanced view than the one law enforcement hand-fed to the media. By then, the story is off the front pages of newspapers and no longer the lead on the broadcast news. In the Liberty City Seven case, for example, four months passed from the day of the indictment before the Miami media were able to interview the primary defendant's wife, who described a very different man from the one presented by the FBI and the Justice Department.[15]

This lack of any immediate doubt on behalf of the media was clear when the Justice Department held a news conference in the U.S. attorney's office in downtown Miami the day after the arrests of the Liberty City Seven. More than two dozen cameras were trained on a lectern crowded with microphones as media liaisons for the Justice Department passed out to reporters copies of a disc with photos of the accused terrorists. At 11:30 a.m.—about thirty minutes after then-Attorney General Alberto Gonzales had finished a news conference in Washington, D.C., in which he said the accused terrorists wanted to wage "a full ground war against the United States"—U.S. Attorney Alex Acosta stood behind the lectern. "We believe that these defendants sought the support of Al Qaeda to, in their own words, wage jihad and war against the United States. To 'kill all the devils that we can,'" Acosta told the gathered reporters. "They hoped that their attacks would be, in their own words, 'just as good or greater than 9/11.'"

Despite the statements of Acosta and Gonzales, reporters didn't have to look hard for information that suggested the Justice Department might be overselling their case. According to the eleven-page indictment, the seven men who supposedly wanted to wage war against the United States didn't have any weapons or explosives, and their only alleged Al Qaeda connection was an FBI informant posing as a terrorist. Even the management company of the Sears Tower, one of the alleged targets, knew the building was never in danger. "This group never got beyond talking about a workable plot," Barbara A. Carley, managing director of the Sears Tower, told the *New York Times* on the day of the press conference. "Federal and local authorities continue to tell us they've never found evidence of a credible terrorism threat against Sears Tower that's ever gone beyond just talk."[16] Yet the reporters at the Miami news conference accepted unchallenged the government's claims that this was an active terrorist group that had sought support from Al Qaeda, which prompted several follow-up questions that the U.S. attorney struggled to answer.

"Was Al Qaeda on its way to responding?" one reporter asked during the press conference. "What kind of feedback did they get?"

"I'm sorry—I don't understand," Acosta replied.

"They asked for money. They asked for weapons. What kind of feedback did they get from Al Qaeda?"

Acosta had to admit reluctantly that the group had never made contact with Al Qaeda. They were in contact with an FBI informant posing as Al Qaeda—that was their crime.

"How did they get the $50,000?" another reporter asked.

"I'm sorry?" Acosta replied.

"You mentioned $50,000," the reporter said, clarifying.

Acosta conceded that while the group did ask for $50,000, they had asked the FBI informant for it, not Al Qaeda, and in the end, they never received any money. The only terrorist involved in the case was an imaginary one on the FBI payroll, a man who called himself Mohammed, and whose real name was Elie Assaad.

The story of how Elie Assaad, Howard Gilbert's fellow informant in the Imran Mandhai case, came to pose once more as an Al Qaeda operative named Mohammed begins with another untrustworthy informant—a five-foot-seven, 190-pound, twenty-one-year-old Yemeni man named Abbas al-Saidi. In 2006, al-Saidi ran a convenience store in North Miami, and one of his frequent customers was Narseal Batiste, a thirty-two-year-old former preacher at a nondenominational Christian church, a father of four, and a one-time Guardian

Angel. Growing up, Batiste had split his time between Chicago and Marksville, a small town in Louisiana. He attended a Catholic high school and his father, Narcisse, a preacher himself, had raised his son to be a Christian. Batiste met his wife, Minerva Vasquez, who was born in Estancia de Animas, a small town in Zacatecas, Mexico, in high school, and Narcisse married them shortly after Vasquez gave birth to her and Batiste's second child, a little girl named Narcassia. Batiste had moved to South Florida following a failed attempt to follow in his father's footsteps as a preacher in Chicago. He also saw Miami as a place to start a new life after his mother, Audrey Batiste, died in 2000 from surgery complications. The youngest of five boys and one girl, Batiste took his mother's sudden death hard. "All my kids took it so hard," remembered Narcisse.[17]

As an adult, Batiste wasn't content in limiting his religious studies to Christian texts, and Islam and the Koran intrigued him particularly—something his father tried to dissuade. "I didn't agree with it, but he was a man by then and I didn't think I could argue with him about it," Narcisse Batiste said.[18] Despite this, Batiste never identified himself as a Muslim. By the time he and his family moved to Miami in 2001, Batiste considered himself a member of the Moorish Science Temple, a religious sect that blends Christianity, Judaism, and Islam. He'd preach to anyone who'd listen and offered martial arts training to disadvantaged, mostly black, kids in Liberty City. He wanted to help clean up Liberty City, and six men—Haitians and African Americans—joined him to form something of a group. Batiste also ran a drywall business, Azteca Stucco and Masonry, out of a run-down warehouse, and his followers were also his employees.

Above all, however, Batiste was a natural-born bullshitter

and hustler. That's how he came to strike up a friendship with the young al-Saidi at the convenience store in North Miami. Batiste, who was trying to keep his drywall business solvent while he and his family were living in a cramped one-bedroom apartment, told al-Saidi he was looking for ways to make money. Al-Saidi said he knew people who could help. "You're always looking for money, and I have some people in Yemen I can introduce you to who would fund your organization, but you gotta spin it the right way, and I'll help you do that," al-Saidi said, according to the story Batiste told his lawyers.

What happened next isn't entirely clear. What is known is that al-Saidi left the United States to visit his wife and family in Yemen and returned on a ticket paid for by the FBI. His task: to infiltrate a terrorist cell in Miami.

Rory J. McMahon sat behind a conference table inside his office in North Fort Lauderdale. It was a fall afternoon in 2009, several years after he had been hired by defense lawyers to investigate Abbas al-Saidi. But the case still bothered him. A private investigator who had previously worked as a federal probation officer, McMahon was asked to piece together how exactly al-Saidi came to be an informant who identified a supposed terrorist cell in the poorest section of Miami. That investigation led McMahon to a public housing project in Brooklyn, New York, and a young woman named Stephanie Jennings, who was al-Saidi's girlfriend. Jennings told McMahon that al-Saidi had been working as an informant for the New York Police Department's Intelligence Division, which since 9/11 has aggressively monitored Muslim communities in New York and New Jersey.[19] For some reason—Jennings was never told why—NYPD handlers became concerned for al-Saidi's safety and moved him and Jennings to a city-funded public housing project. But they didn't stay there long.

One afternoon, one of al-Saidi's friends from the Middle East knocked on the door. Jennings, home alone, let him in, and with al-Saidi not around, the friend raped her in the apartment. Jennings went to the police and pressed charges; when al-Saidi returned home, she told him what happened. "Instead of saying, 'I'm going to go kill the motherfucker,' his response was, 'We can use this to get money,' because she pressed charges," McMahon recalled. "So he goes to the guy. 'Give me $7,000 and I'll get Stephanie to drop the rape charge against you.' So that's what they do, and he uses the $7,000 for seed money to move to Miami."

In South Florida, al-Saidi and Jennings lived in a neatly kept apartment building in Miami Beach, just steps from Biscayne Bay and near the Seventy-Ninth Street Causeway. But their relationship wasn't as neatly kept as their building. On November 10, 2004, Jennings stepped out of the apartment to smoke a cigarette, which annoyed al-Saidi. When she walked back in, the Yemeni man punched her in the left eye and in the stomach, then bit her on the neck.[20] When Jennings, crying, began to complain of pain, al-Saidi called 911. After the police arrived, al-Saidi told them, "I bit her because she choked me!" But the police documented that al-Saidi did not have any bruising to indicate he'd been choked, so they arrested him and charged him with simple battery, a misdemeanor. At the time, al-Saidi told police he was an unemployed laborer.

Stuck in jail, according to a story he would later tell Jennings, al-Saidi called his former contact at the NYPD Intelligence Division.

"Is there anything you can do to help me out?" al-Saidi asked.

"I'm a New York City cop. There's nothing I can do," the detective said. "But I work with some FBI agents, and I'll let them know."

FBI agents working under Miami's Mark Hastbacka then met with al-Saidi. Hastbacka was the agent who supervised the Mandhai investigation as well as a late 1990s case involving Irish Republican Army gun smugglers. What was said or promised to al-Saidi while he was at the Miami-Dade County jail isn't known. But shortly after al-Saidi's meeting with the FBI, he was released from jail and prosecutors dropped the battery charge against him. In less than a year, al-Saidi would call the FBI about an alleged terrorist cell in Miami led by a street preacher named Narseal Batiste. And Hastbacka would have himself another high-profile terrorism case in South Florida.

Though he lived in a one-bedroom apartment and ran a failing drywall business, Narseal Batiste thought of himself as a leader—and as a godlike man. He described himself as the god of his organization and once said he believed that "man has the authority to, on a certain level, be God." He called himself Prince and required his small group of followers to do the same. Batiste's hero was Jeff Fort, a Chicago gang leader who co-founded the Almighty Black P. Stone Nation—a black Islam-influenced organization that was financed through criminal activity and maintained order in Chicago's South Side.[21]

Fort and Batiste had a lot in common. Both were born in the South and raised in Chicago. Both called themselves Prince. While Fort worked to help disadvantaged Chicago communities, Batiste wanted to aid poor Miami neighborhoods. Both identified their religions as offshoots of the Moorish Science Temple, though neither was an official member. Fort's gang would march in Chicago wearing uniforms and kufis, while Batiste and his six followers and drywall employees would exercise on the streets of Liberty City wearing uniforms. And there was one more startling similarity that prosecutors would ultimately use against Batiste to great effect: he and Fort were also both alleged terrorists. In 1987, Fort was convicted of conspiring with Libya to perform acts of terrorism in the United States; he'd offered Muammar Gaddafi his gang's services in exchange for $2.5 million.[22]

Of course, that isn't altogether different from what the U.S. government alleges Batiste did. He believed al-Saidi had a rich uncle in Yemen who would be willing to send money if Batiste and his group would launch an attack in the United States. Talking big, Batiste claimed to have an army of men at the ready in Chicago. "I can get 5,000 soldiers in Chicago," he told al-Saidi. "I used to be a leader of the Blackstone Rangers," he added, referring to Fort's gang. "They would have done any fuckin' thing I told them to do."

"OK, brother. Do you want to go to Chicago?" al-Saidi asked.

"Got to go to Chicago."

"When you want to go?"

"As soon as we get the money. Soon as we get the money."[23]

To get the money, however, Batiste would have to meet an associate of al-Saidi's family. On November 21, 2005, Batiste expressed his concern to the informant about meeting someone new. "We don't know if this guy might be a double agent," he said. "He might work for the FBI."

"No, he just came from back home," al-Saidi said. "I don't believe that, and if I'm getting a trust from my family, from one side, they wouldn't—they wouldn't deal with somebody that was like that. I know them; forget it. From the next side, I'm not gonna do anything until I get to know the person."

"Um-hmm," Batiste said, as if to acknowledge the statement.

"That's why he's coming, so he can get—cause they're saying the same thing," al-Saidi said. "How can he trust these brothers … I know them for a long time, I trust them, so they're like, 'OK.'"

"A person that's coming to—coming to evaluate," Batiste said.

A few minutes later, Batiste asked al-Saidi about the one who would be coming to evaluate them. "So does he know bin Laden?"

"I don't know, brother," al-Saidi said. "Believe me, I don't know."[24]

Just as it had in the Mandhai investigation, the FBI brought in Elie Assaad to serve as a closer halfway through the Liberty City sting after al-Saidi couldn't build a strong enough case to bring to prosecutors. Assaad would again play a terrorist operative named Mohammed. On December 16, 2005, Batiste and Assaad met for the first time. At the meeting, Batiste compared himself to Jeff Fort. Assaad asked Batiste what he needed. In block letters, Batiste scribbled down the following on a Radisson Hotel notepad:

Boots > knee high > ankle boots
Uniforms > black security guard type
Machine guns > automatic hand pistols type
Radio communication. Nextel, Motorola cell phones.
Squad cars > SUV Truck > Black color[25]

The following week, in a conversation on December 21, 2005, Batiste's bragging continued. He told al-Saidi that with some financial help he and his men could launch attacks on buildings throughout the country, including in Chicago. "We need to have the gangs go crazy in the streets," Batiste said. "You see what I'm saying? That will cause a massive confusion."

"But you know, brother—" al-Saidi started.

"Let me tell you something," Batiste continued. "There's two major buildings that blow up. The Empire State Building and the Sears Tower. Sears Tower—it's the tallest building in the world. It used to be the Empire State Building. Then you gotta get—you gotta get the buildings right here in Miami. California, some in Texas. That sounds impossible, but it can be done. It can be done because they can be put on fire. Burn them to the ground. But whatever they take to burn them, whatever they take to destroy them, they gonna have to be destroyed." Not only were Batiste's ideas to take down skyscrapers with his ragtag group of six guys far beyond his capability, but they also suggested his grip on reality wasn't particularly firm. For example, he also told the FBI informant that he believed they could topple the Sears Tower in such a way that it would fall into Lake Michigan and create a tsunami that would destroy parts of Chicago.[26]

Over the next three months, Assaad built up a level of trust with Batiste. But oddly, during this time, Batiste never seemed to know which terrorist organization the informant represented. In a March 16, 2006, conversation, Assaad mentioned that he worked for Osama bin Laden—a fact that surprised Batiste.

"I did not know that, ah, Osama bin Laden was your leader. The great sheikh," Batiste said.

"I—" Assaad started, before being interrupted by Batiste.

"I did not know that."

"You didn't know," Assaad followed.

"I didn't know that, really," Batiste said.

"So because I know you send, you send after Al Qaeda. You send—"

"Well," Batiste interjected.

"You send the message?" Assaad said.

"I just told, ah, I just told Abbas that you know, what I was trying to do and I told them I needed some help. He told me that he knew some people that was fighting in jihad and, and, ah, but there's so many different types of groups that's fighting in jihad, like Hamas and all of them. I thought maybe it was probably one of those."

Assaad also told Batiste that day that he and his men needed to take a *bayat*—a pledge of allegiance to Al Qaeda. As the group's leader, Batiste would need to take the pledge first. But the pledge, recorded and entered into evidence at trial, bore a certain "Who's on First?" flavor:

"*God's pledge is upon me, and so is his compact*," Assaad said as he and Batiste sat in his car. "Repeat after me."

"Okay. *Allah's pledge is upon you.*"

"No, you have to repeat exactly. *God's pledge is upon me, and so is his compact.* You have to repeat."

"Well, I can't say Allah?" Batiste asked.

"Yeah, but this is an English version because Allah, you can say whatever you want, but—"

"Okay. Of course."

"Okay."

"*Allah's pledge is upon me. And so is his compact*," Batiste said, adding: "That means his angels, right?"

"Uh, huh. *To commit myself*," Assaad continued.

"*To commit myself.*"

"*Brother.*"

"*Brother,*" Batiste repeated.

"Uh. That's, uh, what's your, uh, what's your name, brother?"

"Ah, Brother Naz."

"Okay. *To commit myself,*" the informant repeated.

"*To commit myself.*"

"*Brother.*"

"*Brother.*"

"You're not—you have to say your name!" Assaad cried.

"Naz. Naz."

"Uh. To commit myself. I am Brother Naz. You can say, '*To commit myself.*'"

"*To commit myself, Brother Naz.*"

Things then went smoothly for a while until Assaad came to a reference to being "protective of the secrecy of the oath and to the directive of Al Qaeda." Here Batiste stopped. "And to ... what is the directive of?"

"Directive of Al Qaeda," the informant answered.

"So now let me ask you this part here. That means that Al Qaeda will be over us?"

"No, no, no, no, no," Assaad said. "It's an alliance."

"Oh. Well..." Batiste said, sounding resigned.

"It's an alliance, but it's like a commitment, by, uh, like, we respect your rules. You respect our rules," Assaad explained.

"Uh, huh," Batiste mumbled.

"*And to the directive of Al Qaeda,*" Assaad said, waiting for Batiste to repeat.

"Okay, can I say an alliance?" Batiste asked. "*And to the alliance of Al Qaeda?*"

"Of the alliance, of the directive—" Assaad said, catching

himself. "You know what you can say? *And to the directive and the alliance of Al Qaeda.*"

"Okay, *directive and alliance of Al Qaeda*," Batiste said.

"Okay," the informant said. "Now officially you have commitment and we have alliance between each other. And welcome, Brother Naz, to Al Qaeda."[27] Assaad then administered the oath to five of Batiste's six followers—Patrick Abraham, Stanley Phanor, Rotschild Augustine, Burson Augustin, and Naudimar Herrera. (By then, the sixth follower, Lyglenson Lemorin, had left the group.)

After administering the oath, Assaad spoke in front of the group about a secret message from Osama bin Laden. Al Qaeda, Assaad told the men, was planning to blow up five FBI buildings around the country, including the one in Miami, and needed assistance in obtaining videos and photographs of these buildings. Batiste, in turn, requested a van for the surveillance and a memory chip for his personal camera. On March 24, 2006, Batiste and Patrick Abraham drove Assaad to a Circuit City, where he bought a memory chip. They then drove by and identified the FBI building in North Miami Beach, the National Guard armory and a Jewish synagogue.

Throughout all of this, how dedicated Batiste really was to committing an act of terrorism remains questionable. The FBI's undercover recordings suggested that Batiste, who was having trouble paying the rent on his warehouse, was mostly trying to shake down his "terrorist" friend. After first asking the informant for $50,000, Batiste is recorded in conversation after conversation asking how soon he'll have the cash.

"Let me ask you a question," he said in one exchange. "Once I give you an account number, how long do you think it's gonna take to get me something in?"

"So you is scratching my back, [I'm] scratching your

back—we're like this," Assaad dodged.

"Right," Batiste said.[28]

To prove that he had connections in Chicago, Batiste suggested that they fly Charles James Stewart to Miami. Stewart, also known as Sultan Khan Bay, was a convicted rapist and a leader of the Moorish Science Temple in Chicago. He also was affiliated with Jeff Fort's gang, the Almighty Black P. Stone Nation. Assaad gave Batiste $3,500 to fly Stewart and his wife from Chicago. Batiste was able to convince Stewart to come down by saying that they needed him to help them start a Moorish Science Temple in Miami.

In meetings recorded by the FBI, Batiste and Stewart smoked marijuana as they discussed absurd plans, such as opening a shop to sell drugs and building a Moorish nation in the United States. But Stewart's visit to Miami ultimately backfired on Batiste—and the FBI—as the two men began to disagree about the direction of the Miami organization. After Batiste told Stewart about his plans with al-Saidi and Assaad, Stewart told him that he was being duped by FBI informants. Stewart then kicked Batiste out of his own organization and took command of the small group.

The so-called terrorist cell al-Saidi had initially identified was falling apart. A few members sided with Batiste; the others cut off all ties. Master G.J.G. Atheea, one of Batiste's former spiritual advisers, confronted Stewart in Miami to complain about how he had treated Batiste. Whether Atheea did this of his own volition isn't known, as he was also working as an FBI informant at this point. And that's when the Liberty City case gets even stranger. Stewart, angered by being confronted, pulled out a gun and began firing at Atheea, who escaped unharmed. Police then arrested Stewart for possessing a firearm as a convicted felon. Federal prosecutors filed charges, and ultimately Stewart cut a deal to become a government witness against Batiste.

After Stewart's arrest, the FBI raided Batiste's warehouse in Liberty City and federal prosecutors charged him and his followers with conspiracy to support terrorism, destroy buildings, and levy war against the U.S. government.

James J. Wedick, a former FBI supervisory agent who spent more than three decades at the Bureau, was hired to review the Liberty City Seven case as a consultant for the defense. I met with him at his home outside Sacramento, California, in late 2010 and asked him about the case. His first reaction was a smirk. "These guys couldn't find their way down the end of the street," Wedick said of Batiste and his followers. "They were homeless types. And, yes, we did show a picture where somebody was taking the oath to Al Qaeda. So what? They didn't care. They only cared about the money. When we put forth a case like that to suggest to the American public that we're protecting them, we're not protecting them. The agents back in the bullpen, they know it's not true."

Indeed, the Justice Department had a difficult time winning convictions in the Liberty City Seven case. It was clear from trial testimony that Batiste, the alleged ringleader, was merely bullshitting with the FBI informants, free-flowing with absurd ideas he'd picked up from popular culture in the hopes that he might see some cash at the end of the hustle. For example, when his lawyer asked him on the stand how he came up with the idea to bomb the Sears Tower, Batiste answered: "Just from watching the movies."[29] In three separate trials, juries deadlocked on most of the charges, eventually acquitting two of the defendants—Lyglenson Lemorin and

Naudimar Herrera—and convicting the other five of crimes that landed them in prison for between seven and thirteen years.* (To date, Lemorin's and Herrera's acquittals are the exceptions to what is otherwise a perfect conviction record for FBI terrorism sting cases that go to trial.) Despite the eventual convictions, the U.S. government was never able to show in any of the three trials that the Liberty City Seven had the ability to commit an act of terrorism were it not for the FBI informants providing them with the means.

For the Justice Department, the case was an early test of what has become known as preemptive prosecution—when the government uses terrorism conspiracy charges to make the case for what defendants would have done if not busted by federal law enforcement. Liberty City Seven prosecutor Jacqueline Arango emphasized this in her closing arguments. "The government need not wait until buildings come down or people get shot to prove people are terrorists," she said. But if the government doesn't need to show that defendants committed the crime, Batiste's lawyer asked the jury in her closing argument, how can we be sure that they would have committed the crime without the prodding of government informants? "This is not a terrorism case," Ana Jhones told the jury. "This is a manufactured crime."[30]

The Liberty City Seven case, however, proved to be quite

---

*Lemorin, who had left the group before it engaged in an alleged terrorist plot with an FBI informant, was acquitted in the first trial due to lack of evidence and later deported to Haiti. Herrera was unexplainably acquitted in the third trial when the evidence against him was similar to the evidence against the five men in the plot who were convicted. Herrera's not guilty verdict was an anomaly—something none of the jurors has come forward to explain—since his actions weren't significantly different from those of the other defendants.

lucrative for the informants involved in it. Elie Assaad earned $85,000 for his work on the case, while Abbas al-Saidi received $21,000.[31]

Several years later, Elie Assaad resurfaced in El Paso, Texas, where he was running a low-rent modeling agency on the Mexico border. In March 2011, El Paso police attempted to pull over Assaad's black SUV on the interstate. Instead of stopping, Assaad led the police on a high-speed chase through the city and onto the campus of the University of Texas at El Paso, where he drove into a dead end, reversed, and backed into a police officer whose gun was drawn. The officer fired several times. Assaad later rolled his SUV on a nearby street as he tried to get away.[32]

I called Assaad shortly after his arrest and asked if I could meet with him in El Paso. He told me his incredulous story about how he came to serve as an FBI informant and bragged on the phone about how his work as an informant saved the United States from another terrorist attack—but he wouldn't agree to meet with me. He's saving his story, he said, for his own book. He's still looking for a publisher.

Since the 9/11 hijackers spent the days before their attack in hot and balmy Florida, it's fitting that terrorism sting operations were born in the Sunshine State. Starting as an idea from a security guard named Howard Gilbert with big dreams, these stings would have their greatest test in court with the Liberty City Seven case, which proved to the government that it could win terrorism prosecutions even when no evidence linked the defendants to actual terrorists.

J. Stephen Tidwell, the FBI's executive assistant director who supports the use of terrorism sting operations, and James

J. Wedick, the former FBI supervisory agent who is opposed to them, both told me that the FBI and the Justice Department viewed the Liberty City Seven case as a test of what the law and juries would allow in terrorism cases in a post-9/11 United States. Winning the case, even if it did take three trials, strengthened the government's position in using terrorism sting operations. It also sent a message to defense lawyers that the Justice Department can win these cases at trial, and this likely has played a role in the high rate of guilty pleas we see today following terrorism stings.

But that doesn't mean that the government treated the members of the Liberty City Seven like dangerous terrorists after their trial and conviction. One of the convicted men, Burson Augustin, has already been released from prison, and he's back in Florida. While the government portrayed him as a dangerous killer who wanted to bomb buildings in June 2006, when authorities released him in September 2012, they never even bothered to warn the community that a convicted terrorist was living among them, suggesting either that the U.S. government believes terrorists can be fully rehabilitated after short prison sentences, or that those convicted as terrorists weren't really dangerous in the first place.

Augustin is the first man convicted in a post-9/11 terrorism sting operation to be released from prison. During the six years he was incarcerated, the FBI has dramatically stepped up its use of terrorism sting operations. To do that, the Bureau has had to recruit thousands of informants to perform the job of agent provocateur that Howard Gilbert and Elie Assaad helped pioneer. But not every informant has hooked up with the FBI in the hopes of becoming a secret agent man, as Howard Gilbert did, or of becoming a federal snitch for the money, as Elie Assaad did. Many spy for the government because FBI agents have coerced them into doing so. Just as agents have targeted Muslim communities to find terrorists, they have also targeted those same communities to recruit informants, using any means necessary.

4. LEVERAGE

Bush-Cheney and Kerry-Edwards campaign signs littered the lawns in his North Miami Beach neighborhood as Imam Foad Farahi walked from his mosque to his apartment a few blocks away. It was five o'clock in the afternoon on November 1, 2004, the day before George W. Bush would win a second term in office, but Farahi, an influential South Florida Islamic religious leader, had been too busy fasting and praying Ramadan to pay much attention to the presidential election.

As he neared his apartment, he saw two men standing outside. "We're from the FBI," one of the men said. They wanted to know about José Padilla and Adnan El Shukrijumah, two men linked to the Al Qaeda terrorist network. Padilla, the so-called Dirty Bomber, had been arrested in May 2002 and given enemy combatant status. He stood trial in Miami and was convicted in 2008 on terrorism charges and sentenced to seventeen years in prison. Currently on the FBI's most wanted terrorist list, Shukrijumah is a senior Al Qaeda member who came to the Bureau's attention in the Imran Mandhai case.

"I know José Padilla, but I don't know Adnan," Farahi told the agents.[1] As imam of the Shamsuddin Islamic Center in North Miami Beach, Farahi was in a unique position to know about local Muslims. While he had met Shukrijumah, the son of a local Islamic religious leader, on one occasion in 2000, he had had no contact with him since then. "I don't know anything about his activities," Farahi said. Padilla had prayed at Farahi's mosque and had once been among his Arabic students. However, Farahi told the agents that he had had "no contact with Padilla since 1998, when he left the country."

"We want you to work with us," one of the agents then said to Farahi.

"I have no problem working with you guys or helping you out," Farahi told the agents. He could keep them informed about the local Muslim community, or translate Arabic. But the relationship, he insisted, would need to be made public; others would have to know he was working with the government. But that wasn't what the FBI had in mind: the agents wanted him to become a secret informant. And they knew Farahi was in a vulnerable position as his student visa had expired and he had asked the government for a renewal. He had also applied for political asylum, hoping one of those legal tracks would offer a way for him to stay in the United States indefinitely.

"We'll give you residency," the agents promised. "We'll give you money to go to school."

Farahi considered the offer for a moment, then shook his head. "I can't," he told them.

The slender, bearded Farahi frowned as he recounted this to me while sitting on a white folding chair in the Shamsuddin Islamic Center in May 2009. "People trust you as a religious figure, and you're trying to kind of deceive them," he said, remembering the choice he faced. "That's where the problem is."

Farahi soon discovered that the FBI's offer wasn't optional, as the federal government began using strong-arm tactics—including trying to have him deported and falsely claiming it had information linking him to terrorism—in an effort to force him to become an informant. The imam resisted the government at every step of the way and took his political asylum case to the U.S. Court of Appeals in Atlanta. "As long as you're not a citizen, there are lots of things [the government] can do," Ira Kurzban, Farahi's lawyer, told me.[2] "They can allege you're a terrorist and try to bring terrorist charges against you, or they can get you deported."

Farahi's was among the first cases to become public of the FBI using leverage to recruit informants from within U.S. Muslim communities, an aggressive program that has netted thousands of informants since 9/11. And the only reason his case became public was because Farahi chose to fight, risking deportation. "People have two choices," Farahi told me. "Either they end up working with the FBI or they leave the country on their own. It's just sometimes when you're in that situation, not many people are strong enough to stand up and resist and fight—to reject their offers."

Two days after Farahi told the FBI he couldn't spy on members of his mosque in good conscience, the two agents phoned him and requested he come to their office to take a polygraph. "I had nothing to hide," Farahi said of the test. "They asked the same questions over and over, to see if my answer would change, and it didn't." The agents were focused primarily on Adnan El Shukrijumah, Farahi recalled. "What is your relationship with him?" they asked. "When was the last time you were in contact with him? Where is he now?"

Following the polygraph, Farahi didn't hear from the FBI for two and a half years. Then, in the summer of 2007, he received a call from an agent who asked to meet with him. In Cooper City, a suburb northwest of Miami, two FBI agents—

a man and a woman—again asked Farahi if he would work with the government. He again declined, and the meeting ended amicably.

Farahi didn't know the push back would come later on.

Though he has never set foot in the country, Foad Farahi is technically an Iranian. He was born in Kuwait, but under Middle Eastern law, he is considered an Iranian citizen because his father was from there. Farahi grew up in Kuwait City, where his father operated a currency exchange business. His mother, a Syrian, raised him and his younger sister to speak Arabic and worship as Sunnis, an Islamic sect that is persecuted in Iran. But he knew his future would never be secure in Kuwait. "Even if I married a Kuwaiti woman, I wouldn't become a citizen," Farahi said. "Kuwait could deport me to Iran at any time for any reason."

At the age of nineteen, Farahi applied for and received a student visa to study in the United States. He chose to go to South Florida, where his family had once vacationed when he was a teenager. He enrolled at Miami Dade College and received an associate's degree before transferring to Barry University, a private Catholic school in Miami Shores, where he earned a bachelor's degree in chemistry. While at Barry, he served on the university's interfaith committee as well as participating as a teacher in a university peace forum attended by Jewish, Christian, and Muslim children. "He has had a positive influence at this university," said Edward R. Sunshine, a theology professor at Barry.[3] No one who knows Farahi, Sunshine told me, would suspect he is radical or militant.

Farahi went on to obtain a master's degree in public health from Florida International University. At the same time, he began an intensive, three-year imam training course at a mosque in Miramar, Florida. In 2000, the Shamsuddin Islamic Center opened near his home in North Miami Beach. Six months later, its imam returned to Egypt, and Farahi became his successor. It was through this position that he came into contact with several South Floridians who have been linked to terrorism, including Padilla, Shukrijumah, and Imran Mandhai, the nineteen-year-old Pakistani American man who conspired with FBI informants Howard Gilbert and Elie Assaad. "Imran came here once years ago during Ramadan," Farahi said. "It was a big event for him at the time. He memorized and recited the Koran."

On a November day in 2007, Farahi arrived at Miami Immigration Court for what he thought was a routine hearing on his political asylum case. The imam had requested asylum because he is a Sunni, a persecuted religious minority in Iran. As Farahi entered the courthouse, he saw four men from U.S. Immigration and Customs Enforcement (ICE). They were wearing body armor and had guns holstered at their sides. All four followed Farahi from the security checkpoint on the ground level to the third-floor courtroom of U.S. Immigration Judge Carey Holliday.

Farahi's lawyer at the time, Mildred Morgado, spoke with the ICE agents, then asked to talk to her client in private. "They have a file with evidence that you're supporting or are involved in terrorist groups," Farahi recalled Morgado telling him. Farahi was then given an ultimatum: drop the asylum case and leave the United States voluntarily, or be charged as a terrorist.

Unfortunately, luck wasn't on Farahi's side when drawing a judge for his asylum claim. Appointed to the immigration court in October 2006, Carey Holliday was a Louisiana Republican who had quickly earned a reputation for being tough on immigrants. In one case, he declined to hear arguments from an Ecuadorian couple who alleged they were targeted for deportation because their daughter, Miami Dade College student Gabby Pacheco, was a well-known activist for immigration reform. "People who live in glass houses should not throw stones," Holliday wrote in his ruling.[4] (Holliday resigned in January 2009 after the Justice Department found that Bush administration officials had illegally selected immigration judges based on their political affiliation.)

After the ICE agents threatened Farahi with terrorism charges, he told Holliday he would voluntarily leave the country within thirty days. Although his Iranian passport was expired—a bureaucratic problem that should have given him more time to consider the government's threat—Holliday granted the order of voluntary departure. The agents let Farahi go free after he promised to leave the country. However, Farahi later changed his mind and decided to appeal the government's action, as he believed that the claim that Justice Department lawyers would prosecute him as a terrorist was a bluff—nothing more than leverage to coerce him into becoming an informant. To this day, the government has never shared with Farahi or his lawyer any information about the professed evidence that he is a terrorist, and he has never been charged with a crime. "If they have something on Foad, they should make it public. They haven't done that," said Sunshine, the Barry University theology professor. "They are intimidating and bullying, and I resent that type of behavior being paid for by my tax dollars."

Farahi's assertion that the government tried to coerce him to become an informant could not be verified independently because the FBI won't comment on his case. "It is a matter of policy that we do not confirm or deny who we have asked to be a source," Miami FBI Special Agent Judy Orihuela told me. However, other individuals whom the FBI wanted to use as informants have been targeted in a similar manner as Farahi. In November 2005, for example, immigration officials questioned Yassine Ouassif, a twenty-four-year-old Moroccan, as he crossed into New York State from Canada. The officials confiscated his green card and instructed him to meet an FBI agent in Oakland, California. The Bureau's offer: become an informant or be deported. Ouassif refused to spy and won his deportation case with the help of the National Legal Sanctuary for Community Advancement, a nonprofit that advocates for civil rights on behalf of Muslims and immigrants from the Middle East and South Asia.

Another case involves Brooklyn religious leader Sheikh Tarek Saleh, who has been fighting deportation since refusing to become an informant against his estranged cousin, Mustafa Abu al-Yazid, the Egyptian-born man the 9/11 Commission identified as Al Qaeda's "chief financial manager." Even after al-Yazid was killed in a Predator drone strike in Pakistan in early 2010, the government continued to press for Saleh's deportation, alleging that the religious leader had lied on his visa application about never having been part of a terrorist group.[5] Saleh had once been a member of the Egyptian Islamic Jihad—but his membership had been years before the U.S. government had designated the group as a terrorist organization. Saleh has alleged in court documents that the government is retaliating against him for refusing to be an informant. The Council on American-Islamic Relations suspects there are hundreds of similar cases in which the government has used deportation or criminal charges to force cooperation from informants. Unlike Farahi's, Ouassif's, and Saleh's, most of these cases will never be made public.

For his part, Foad Farahi continues to maintain that he is not affiliated with any terrorist groups, and that he would report any Muslim who was supporting terrorism to the authorities. "From the Islamic perspective, it's your duty to respect the law, and if there's anything going on, any crime about to be committed, or any kind of harm to be caused to people or property, it should be reported to the police," he said.

Ira Kurzban's law office is a mile from the alfresco restaurants of Miami's Coconut Grove. It was a hot day in late August 2009 when I met with him, and he was wearing a white guayabera and looking disheveled gray hairs. Kurzban is a well-known advocate for immigrants' rights, having argued three immigration-related cases before the U.S. Supreme Court. He is also on the board of directors of Immigrants' List, the first political action committee in Washington, D.C., established to support candidates who endorse immigration reform. Foad Farahi, desperate not to leave the country but frightened after government agents threatened to charge him as a terrorist, hired Kurzban in 2007 to take his case on appeal. "He's an imam in his mosque," Kurzban said of Farahi as he threw his hands in the air in a sort of protest. "He's basically, you know, the rabbi."

In November 2007, Kurzban asked the Board of Immigration Appeals to throw out Farahi's voluntary departure order and reopen his political asylum case, arguing that the imam had been illegally intimidated by the government. The board denied the request, so Kurzban petitioned the U.S. Court of Appeals in Atlanta, which agreed that Farahi's case should be reopened. "The government has many weapons in its arsenal in terms of seeking to remove somebody from the country, and in his case, they were using it, in my view, as leverage to try to get him to cooperate with them or be an informant for them, and when he wouldn't do it, they applied the penalty," Kurzban said. "When it looked like, well, even if he doesn't cooperate with us, he may be able to get away with seeking political asylum, they show up at the hearing and say, 'If you do that, we're going to arrest you now. We just want you out of the country.' I think the real issue is, does the government have the right to do that, to pressure people in that way to make them informants? But I think that's what's going on," Kurzban continued. "It's clearly the modus operandi of the FBI to (a) recruit people who are going to be informants and (b) to use whatever leverage they can to get them to be informants."

The end of Ramadan in September 2009 signaled the five-year anniversary since the FBI had first approached Foad Farahi. Dressed in khaki pants and a white button-down shirt, Farahi walked barefoot through his mosque as members began to arrange food on folding banquet tables. After sundown, everyone would eat and drink together to break the fast. Farahi was distracted as he waved to attendees and hugged others entering the mosque. I asked him if his legal fight with the U.S. government had made him bitter. "I'm not bitter," he answered. "I wouldn't say I'm bitter at all. But I'm tired. I want to live my life in this country. I want to stay here. That's all."

Farahi's political asylum case has so far been unsuccessful, and in late 2012, he applied for residency based on his recent marriage to a U.Sc citizen.

To coerce people into becoming informants, the FBI must exploit vulnerabilities, and the greatest vulnerability in U.S.

Muslim communities today, as the Farahi case shows, is immigration. Sixty-three percent of Muslims in the United States are first-generation immigrants, and forty-five percent of all Muslims in the country have immigrated here since 1990.[6] Through increased interagency coordination, the FBI has access to officials at U.S. Immigration and Customs Enforcement. Therefore, when an agent has someone who is reluctant to become an informant, he or she can turn to colleagues at ICE and inquire about that person's immigration status. Together, they can comb through the individual's personal information as they search for any kind of immigration violation—such as, in the case of Foad Farahi, how he was three credit hours shy of being a full-time student when his visa required him to carry nine graduate credit hours per semester—and then use that violation as leverage to force cooperation. If the immigrant chooses to cooperate, the FBI will tell the court that he is a valuable asset, averting deportation; if the immigrant chooses not to work as an informant, as Farahi did, the FBI will not support him, and the person may face deportation.

Officially, the FBI denies that it uses the threat of deportation as leverage against possible informants. "We are prohibited from using threats or coercion," FBI spokesperson Kathleen Wright told me when I asked her about this form of pressure. But the FBI does acknowledge that it assists helpful informants when they appear in U.S. Immigration Court. "There have been instances when an individual with immigration issues has assisted in investigations and/or been willing to share information," Wright said. "While we do not have the authority to make deportation or immigration decisions, we can advise immigration authorities of the level of cooperation for whatever use they deem appropriate."

In other words, work as an informant and the FBI will help stop you from being deported; refuse and the FBI won't use its considerable influence in court to prevent the issuing of a one-way ticket out of the country.

Immigration violations aren't the only type of pressure that the FBI uses to coerce reluctant informants. Another tried-and-true method the Bureau uses to flip people is the threat of criminal charges. When the FBI aggressively pursued Italian American organized crime in the 1980s, informants were critical to infiltrating these sophisticated, hierarchal organizations. Often, agents were able to use a crime—such as car theft or fraud—to pressure lower-level Mafiosi to become informants. However, there is one key difference between organized crime soldiers and members of Muslim American communities, namely that the latter aren't nearly as likely to break the law. Not only are devout Muslims religiously bound not to violate society's laws, but U.S. Muslims are often of such affluence that they are an improbable group to be involved in serious crime, particularly in comparison to organized crime figures. In the year after 9/11, for example, 26 percent of Muslims in the United States earned more than $100,000 annually, according to a Cornell University study.[7] Go to any mosque in this country, and you're more likely to find an expensive Mercedes in the parking lot than a rusted-out Chevy.

Yet another form of leverage that the FBI uses to recruit reluctant informants is "trash covers," which is the practice of searching through someone's garbage—without obtaining a warrant—in order to uncover incriminating or embarrassing information. Although the FBI has performed trash covers for decades, the Justice Department officially blessed the practice in approving the most recent Domestic Investigations and Operations Guide, which specifically allows federal agents to go through people's trash.[8] The FBI's search for incriminating or embarrassing information isn't limited to people's physical trash, however. More and more, agents are searching publicly accessible databases on social networks—Facebook, Google+, and Twitter, for example—to mine digital cast offs that could provide information about individuals who are reluctant to become informants.

For agents working counterterrorism investigations, informants are critical, and applying leverage—from immigration violations to criminal charges to even something as personal as extramarital relationships—is the best, and sometimes only, way to recruit informants. "We could go to a source and say, 'We know you're having an affair. If you work with us, we won't tell your wife,'" a former top FBI counterterrorism official told me, asking that he not be identified because he wasn't authorized to discuss informant recruitment on the record. "Would we actually call the wife if the source doesn't cooperate? Not always. You do get into ethics here—is this the right thing to do?—but the legality of this isn't a question. If you obtained the information legally, then you can use it however you want."

It's an oppressive prospect that the full power of a federal law enforcement agency could be directed at someone not even suspected of having committed a crime, but FBI agents are quick to defend the search for information that can be leveraged in the recruitment of snitches. Mike Rolince, a retired FBI agent who spent thirty-one years at the Bureau and specialized in counterterrorism, is among the defenders of this practice. I asked Rolince if he thought the Bureau was going too far today in trying to leverage cooperation from informants in Muslim American communities. He told me that he didn't think the fact that the FBI applied pressure to informants was a problem by itself. Instead, he said, the problem was the perception that the FBI does so willy-nilly and frequently. "The reality at the end of the day is that these tactics are used sparingly," Rolince told me. "Maybe Italian Americans felt offended we went after John Gotti and recruited informants in Italian communities. But we needed to do that then, just as we need to recruit informants in Muslim communities today."

While the threat of deportation is the prime weapon the FBI uses to coerce would-be informants, that tactic has its limitations, as it cannot be used against people who are already U.S. citizens. In those situations, the Bureau relies on other pressure points, the most prominent of which is putting someone on the government's no-fly list. Maintained by the Terrorist Screening Center, an FBI group charged with identifying suspected or potential terrorists, the no-fly list prevents an individual from boarding a flight in the United States. Created after 9/11, the list has an infamous history of false positives—the late Senator Edward Kennedy of Massachusetts was repeatedly stopped at airports, for example, because the vague name "T. Kennedy" was on the list—and at one point even Nobel Peace Prize winner and former South African president Nelson Mandela made the list, a problem then-Secretary of State Condoleezza Rice described to a 2008 Senate committee as "frankly a rather embarrassing matter."[9]

In spite of these high-profile incidents, since at least 2010, the FBI has used the no-fly list as a tool for coercing cooperation from would-be Muslim informants who are American citizens. As an example, one of the FBI's informant recruitment efforts focused on Ibraheim "Abe" Mashal, a thirty-one-year-old living in St. Charles, Illinois, with his wife and three children. Mashal, who was honorably discharged from the U.S. Marine Corps in 2003, was working as a dog trainer with clients in twenty-three states when he received a call from a woman in Spokane, Washington, asking him to come work with her dog. The woman agreed to pay for an airplane ticket, hotel, and fee for Mashal—a typical arrangement for him. On April 20, 2010, Mashal arrived at Chicago's Midway Airport for a flight to Spokane, only to be turned away by the ticketing agent, who told him he was on the no-fly list.

FBI agents later arranged to interview Mashal, and he assumed the embarrassing affair was a mix-up that the agents would sort out. But that didn't happen. Instead, on June 23, 2010, Mashal received a call from an FBI agent. "We've got good news," Mashal remembered being told.[10] "Meet us at Embassy Suites." The hotel wasn't far from his home, and when he arrived at the room, Mashal found two FBI agents sitting in chairs, with a spread of cold cuts and cheese on the table. The agents explained to Mashal that he'd come to their attention after sending emails to a religious cleric in the Middle East whom they were monitoring.

"So you guys were in my email?" Mashal asked the agents.

"We cannot confirm or deny," one of them responded.

Mashal told the agents he knew exactly what they were referring to and was up front about what he had written in the emails. Mashal, whose wife is Christian, had sought an imam's advice on raising children in an interfaith home. "You obviously read the emails," he told the agents. "It was about stuff that has nothing to do with terrorism at all."

The agents didn't respond to the fact that the emails were innocuous, Mashal said. Instead, they asked him if he would like to help them out by providing information about a large suburban Chicago mosque. If he would work as a paid informant for the FBI, the agents told him, the government would remove his name from the no-fly list. "We have informants in your mosque. We have informants in Ann Arbor mosques. We have informants all over the Midwest," Mashal remembered one of the FBI agents telling him.

"Even if I wanted a position like that, I don't have the time. I don't even speak Arabic," Mashal told the agents in response. He then asked to have a lawyer present, and the FBI agents ended the meeting.

Mashal, who to his knowledge is still on the no-fly list, is now one of fifteen plaintiffs in an ACLU lawsuit filed in Oregon against Attorney General Eric Holder and the directors of the FBI and the Terrorist Screening Center for misuse of the no-fly list. "Thousands of people have been barred altogether from commercial air travel without any opportunity to confront or rebut the basis for their inclusion, or apparent inclusion, on a government watch list," the ACLU complaint alleges.[11] "Some of them may be on the list as a result of mistaken identity, but for others, there seems to be this McCarthy-era naming of names going on," Nusrat Choudhury, one of the ACLU lawyers working on the case, told me. "The problem is that there is no way to stand up for yourself, to petition to have your name removed from the list. For that reason, it's the perfect bargaining chip in FBI and law enforcement investigations."[12]

In addition to the no-fly list, another way that the FBI coerces U.S. citizens to become informants is the threat of criminal prosecution. In what has become an embarrassing case for the FBI, the Justice Department in February 2009 charged Ahmadullah Sais Niazi, a naturalized U.S. citizen from Afghanistan who was living in Orange County, California, with lying

in order to obtain citizenship. Niazi, whose estranged brother-in-law was at one time Osama bin Laden's bodyguard in
Afghanistan, came to the FBI's attention as part of an undercover operation code-named Operation Flex, the purpose
of which was to gather intelligence and recruit informants
in Orange and Los Angeles counties. The main actor in the
operation was a well-muscled forty-nine-year-old informant
with a shaved scalp named Craig Monteilh, a convicted felon
who had made his money ripping off cocaine dealers before
becoming an asset for the DEA and later the FBI, for which
he had posed in previous investigations as a white supremacist, a Russian hit man, and a Sicilian drug trafficker.[13]

In Operation Flex, the FBI asked Monteilh to pose as a
French-Syrian Muslim named Farouk al-Aziz and search for
information—such as immigration problems, extramarital
relationships, criminal activities, and drug use—that might
help the Bureau pressure local Muslims into becoming informants. "They wanted information that they could use to
blackmail people," Monteilh told me in 2011.[14] Monteilh
also claimed that the FBI encouraged him to use any means
necessary—including engaging in sexual relationships with
women—to engender trust in the communities he was tasked
with infiltrating.

During the course of the investigation, Monteilh met
Niazi, and once the FBI realized that the Orange County
man had a distant connection to Osama bin Laden, they
asked Monteilh to get close to him. Monteilh became so aggressive in talking about terrorism, however, that Niazi told
the Los Angeles chapter of the Council on American-Islamic Relations about the conversations. A representative from
the organization, in turn, reported Monteilh to the FBI as a
possible terrorist. Just as Monteilh was being exposed, police

in Irvine, California, charged him with bilking two women out of $157,000 as part of an alleged scam. He had asked the women to front him money for human growth hormone, with the promise that he could double their money. But there were no drugs, and the women lost their cash to Monteilh, who pleaded guilty to a grandtheft charge and served eight months in prison. Monteilh claimed the human growth hormone transaction was part of an FBI investigation, and after the FBI failed to have the charges removed, as Monteilh said he had been promised, the informant went public and exposed Operation Flex. He also filed a lawsuit against the FBI and began cooperating with the ACLU in a civil rights complaint against the U.S. government.

After Monteilh was sidelined, the FBI tried to recruit Niazi as an informant, threatening to charge him with lying in answers to a host of questions on his naturalization application, including, among other things, about whether he'd used other names or had connections to terrorist organizations. Once Niazi refused to be an informant, the Justice Department filed the charges. Ultimately, though, just as Operation Flex had, the prosecution against Niazi imploded—primarily due to Monteilh's poisoning of the case through comments he made to the press—and in October 2010, prosecutors dropped the charges against the Orange County man. Niazi has stated publicly that he believes his prosecution was in retaliation for his refusal to work with the government.

Others who have refused to cooperate with the FBI haven't been so fortunate. Tarek Mehanna is one of them. A resident of Sudbury, Massachusetts, Mehanna has a doctorate from the Massachusetts College of Pharmacy and Health Sciences, and no criminal record. After FBI agents failed to persuade Mehanna to become an informant, however, the government charged him with making a false statement, alleging that Mehanna told FBI agents that his friend Daniel Maldonado was in Egypt when Mehanna knew he was in Somalia attending a terrorist training camp. Evidence collected during the FBI investigation found that Mehanna had traveled to Yemen when he was twenty-one years old in an unsuccessful attempt to find a terrorist training camp. Mehanna, who never came into contact with terrorists in Yemen or in the United States, seemed fascinated with extremist texts and jihadi videos. He translated "Thirty-Nine Ways to Serve and Participate in Jihad" and posted it online through Al-Tibyan Publications, a company which has not been linked to Al Qaeda or any of its affiliates. (The text is widely available online in Arabic and English, including on the Internet Archive.) Mehanna also distributed a video online showing the mutilation of the remains of two U.S. soldiers, which may have been done in retaliation for the rape of a young Iraqi girl. When asked by a friend if the legal system could have been used instead to bring justice to the raped girl, Mehanna answered: "Who cares? Texas BBQ is the way to go."[15]

In November 2008, the FBI arrested Mehanna in Massachusetts, where prosecutors charged him with lying to the FBI, for allegedly providing false information about Maldonado's travels. He was also charged with providing material support to a terrorist organization. While Mehanna awaited trial, authorities kept him in solitary confinement and limited his communications. I therefore had to correspond with him through letters. In one dated October 19, 2010, Mehanna described to me how federal authorities tried to coerce him into becoming an informant:

There were explicit threats that if I refused to work as a confidential informant, I would be charged with material support for terrorism. Essentially, everything I am going through now is an implementation of the threats they directed towards me that day. Their exact words were: 'We can do this the easy way'—i.e., I work for them—'or we can see you in court. You have a lot to think about.' Then they left. A few months later, I was arrested and charged not with terrorism, but with the false statement regarding Maldonado. I was allowed out on bail for that charge for the majority of 2009. Towards the middle of September '09, they approached me one more time through a friend, sending me the message that I had 'one last chance,' or things would get worse. A month later, October 21, 2009, you know what happened. And here I am today.

During his trial in late 2011, which included thirty-one days of testimony, federal prosecutors told the jury that Mehanna had traveled to Yemen in 2004 to train with terrorists but failed to locate a training camp. After returning home, prosecutors said, Mehanna conspired with Al Qaeda to promote jihad on the Internet. He was, they said, part of Al Qaeda's "media wing"—in spite of the fact that the government did not provide any evidence directly linking Mehanna to the terrorist organization. Following ten hours of deliberation, a jury found him guilty of conspiring to support Al Qaeda, never specifying whether the jurors found him guilty of supporting terrorists by traveling to Yemen—where he never located any terrorists—or by posting extremist literature on the Internet, material which wasn't even written by terrorists.

Since most of the evidence prosecutors presented dealt

with Mehanna's watching jihadi videos, discussing suicide bombings, translating texts freely available on the web, and researching the 9/11 attackers, civil liberties groups characterized his conviction as a setback for the First Amendment. "It's official," wrote Nancy Murray, education director of the ACLU of Massachusetts, in a guest editorial in the *Boston Globe*. "There is a Muslim exemption to the First Amendment."[16] Andrew F. March, an associate professor of political science at Yale University who specializes in Islamic law, described the Mehanna case in a *New York Times* opinion piece as "one of the most important free speech cases we have seen since *Brandenburg v. Ohio* in 1969."[17] In that case, Clarence Brandenburg, a Ku Klux Klan leader in rural Ohio, gave an inflammatory speech that was recorded during a KKK rally in 1964. Ohio prosecutors charged him under a 1919 state law that prohibited advocating, among other acts, "unlawful methods of terrorism as a means of accomplishing industrial or political reform." Brandenburg was convicted and sentenced to one year in prison. His appeal went to the U.S. Supreme Court in 1969, and in a landmark decision, the justices voted unanimously to overturn Brandenburg's conviction, writing that the government cannot punish speech unless it is intended and likely to result in "imminent lawless action." The type of speech Mehanna engaged in wasn't very different from Brandenburg's, but prosecutors in his trial were able to get around the Supreme Court precedent by claiming that Mehanna's advocacy of Al Qaeda and violence represented material support to the terrorist organization, which was involved in imminent lawless action, lending support to Nancy Murray's provocative claim that there is a Muslim exemption to the First Amendment.

At his sentencing on April 12, 2012, Mehanna addressed U.S. District Judge George A. O'Toole in an eloquent speech that emphasized his belief that he was not a terrorist but rather the victim of a vengeful prosecution for his refusal to be an FBI informant:

> I was approached by two federal agents. They said that I had a choice to make: I could do things the easy way, or I could do them the hard way. The "easy" way, as they explained, was that I would become an informant for the government, and if I did so I would never see the inside of a courtroom or a prison cell. As for the hard way, this is it. Here I am, having spent the majority of the four years since then in a solitary cell the size of a small closet, in which I am locked down for twenty-three hours each day. The FBI and these prosecutors worked very hard—and the government spent millions of tax dollars—to put me in that cell, keep me there, put me on trial, and finally to have me stand here before you today to be sentenced to even more time in a cell.[18]

Judge O'Toole, unmoved by Mehanna's statement, sentenced the twenty-nine-year-old to seventeen years in prison. Mehanna's lawyers have filed an appeal.

For every Foad Farahi, Sheikh Tarek Saleh, Yassine Ouassif, Ahmadullah Sais Niazi, or Tarek Mehanna who resisted FBI pressure to become spies in their communities, there are hundreds of cases—most of which we will never hear about—in which the Bureau succeeded in exerting enough pressure to turn resistant Muslims into informants. Overall, these aggressive tactics have been very effective for the FBI, helping swell the informant ranks to more than 15,000, the largest number in the history of the Bureau. However, the FBI's actions have come with a heavy price, as they have alienated Muslims throughout the United States, with many reporting they are hesitant to talk to federal law enforcement for fear they might be targeted for recruitment as informants. Muslim Advocates, a San Francisco-based civil rights group, distributes a video online that counsels Muslims not to talk to an FBI agent without a lawyer present and never to allow agents into private residences without a search warrant. "If you are contacted by law enforcement, don't answer any questions beyond giving your name," the video instructs.[19] In mosques around the country, newcomers are met with a suspicion that didn't exist before 9/11—a particularly sad state of affairs, as for centuries mosques had been considered welcoming places for strangers and travelers, a tradition that dates back to the nomadic tribes of the Middle East and the earliest days of Islam. "Every Muslim I know just assumes that the person praying next to them is an informant," Hussam Ayloush, the executive director of the Los Angeles chapter of the Council on American-Islamic Relations (CAIR), told me in 2010.

This frayed relationship between Muslim communities and the FBI has resulted in a restricted flow of voluntary information from these communities to federal law enforcement, contrary to the Bureau's rationale for using informants in the first place. Muslims today see FBI agents as potential enemies, not as neighbors with a mutual interest in keeping the local community safe from harm. This means that credible and actionable tips from within Muslim communities—from the people with the best vantage points to see early problems or threats—are going unreported, as Muslim

Americans are afraid that providing information to the FBI will make them the subjects of investigations or candidates for recruitment as informants. "It has a chilling effect on our ability to work with the FBI," said Farhana Khera, executive director of Muslim Advocates and the National Association of Muslim Lawyers.[20] Instead of going directly to the FBI, Muslims today are more likely to pass on any information about threats in their communities through a third-party organization, such as CAIR. When Ahmadullah Sais Niazi suspected that undercover FBI informant Craig Monteilh might be a terrorist, for example, he didn't call the Bureau directly but instead gave the information to CAIR's Hussam Ayloush, who then reported it to the FBI.

The irony in this is that, as a result of aggressively recruiting informants in Muslim communities when the goal of increasing the amount of information available to its agents, the FBI is receiving even fewer credible tips, since very little of the information flowing to federal law enforcement from Muslim communities today is of a non-coerced nature. This is in spite of the fact that data suggests that Muslim Americans would be valuable partners for law enforcement if they felt comfortable talking to agents, since the interests and values of Muslims in this country are nearly identical to those of the general U.S. population. A 2011 study by the Pew Research Center for People and the Press, which interviewed more than 1,000 Musli Americans nationwide, found that Muslims in the United States reject religious extremism by large margins; that 70 percent of Muslim Americans who were born outside of the country become U.S. citizens, a much higher citizenship rate than in other immigrant groups; and that more than half believe Muslims come to the United States in order to adopt American customs and ways of life.[21] The Pew data also shows that Muslims would not tolerate violent extremists in their communities any more than, say, Christians or Jews would. Yet because of the FBI's dragnet approach in Muslim communities, there is less willingness among Muslims to report a tip to the FBI than there is in other religious communities, meaning that the Bureau's alienation of Muslim communities is stifling the very flow of information its agents are working to increase through their aggressive and widespread use of informants.

As a result, instead of local businessmen or community and religious leaders voluntarily providing information to the FBI about suspicious people worshipping in their mosques or living in their neighborhoods, the FBI now relies on coerced informants to provide this information. The credibility of the information these sources offer is questionable, particularly when compared to the potential value of information coming from people with families, businesses, and vested interests in their communities. FBI informants have vested interests too, of course, but they do not include the health and safety of local Muslim communities. They are instead primarily interested in money and working off criminal charges, as was perhaps most evident in Albany, New York, where federal agents used fraud and immigration charges to recruit as a snitch an accused murderer from Pakistan who would become an FBI terrorism superinformant.

5. THE SUPERINFORMANT

Mohammed Hossain, an immigrant from Bangladesh, had made a nice life for himself in the United States. A short, slender man with a long gray beard, Hossain had immigrated to Albany, New York, in 1985 with most of his family—his mother and father, his wife and her mother, and Kyum, his mentally disabled younger brother. Hossain supported all of them by owning and operating the Little Italy Pizzeria on Central Avenue in Albany. Finding good help in Albany was difficult, so Hossain often did every job in the restaurant himself, including delivery. He and his family lived in a modest apartment above the pizzeria.

When he wasn't rushing around town dropping off pizzas, Hossain was buying run-down properties at municipal auctions, fixing them up, and then renting them out. He always paid cash, and owing to his frugal nature, Hossain would buy doors and fixtures and anything else the houses needed at secondhand stores. By 2003, at the age of fifty, and after less than two decades in the United States, Hossain had accumulated real estate valued at nearly $1 million.

But Hossain's dream life in the United States quickly turned into a nightmare when a visitor arrived at his pizzeria one afternoon in November 2003. Hossain was walking back to Little Italy after having delivered a pizza when he passed his children on the sidewalk, playing with small toy helicopters.

"Who gave you these toys?" Hossain asked his kids.[1]

"Uncle," they replied, explaining that the man who gave them the helicopters said he was Hossain's brother from Bangladesh. Hossain knew that this was impossible, however, as his brother didn't have a visa, so there was no way he could be in the United States. Hossain thought it odd that a stranger would not only give his children toy helicopters, but then claim to be a faraway uncle the children had never met.

The following day, as he entered the pizzeria, Hossain saw an unfamiliar man standing in the corner. He was tall and slender, with a fair complexion, dark brown eyes, and neatly trimmed black hair. He was the person, Hossain would soon discover, who had given his children the toy helicopters.

"Brother, you don't know me, but I know you," the man said, giving his name as Malik. He said he was from Pakistan, and that he owned a gas station and convenience store in town. He told Hossain that he'd heard that the Little Italy Pizzeria was for sale.

"I had wanted to sell it," Hossain answered, "but that was a long time ago." At one point, a community member had offered to buy Little Italy, but the sale had fallen through. He wasn't actively looking for a buyer, Hossain told his new acquaintance, but if someone offered him the right price for the business, he'd sell it.

Just then, Hossain's brother Kyum came in from the kitchen. Kyum was in his thirties, but he had the intellect of a five-year-old and spoke only limited Bengali. Malik called Kyum over and told Hossain he could arrange to get Kyum a driver's license, explaining that he was a translator who helped immigrants obtain driver's licenses.

"My brother doesn't even know how to hold a driving wheel," Hossain said. "He could cause a lot of problems on the road. However, if you want to help him, then give him an ID card, because he has gotten lost on several occasions." Indeed, Kyum's wandering had been a problem for the family. Once, after seeing a plane fly over Little Italy, Kyum decided he wanted to see airplanes up close and, without telling Hossain, walked to Albany International Airport. When he arrived, he was tired, thirsty, and hungry and didn't have any money, so he started grabbing food out of people's hands. The police arrested Kyum, but without any identification on him—he had forgotten his green card—they were forced to lock him up as a John Doe. Several days later, the authorities figured out who he was and called Hossain. It took immigration officials several weeks to return Kyum, a legal resident but not a citizen, to his family. That was why Hossain thought it would be a good idea for Kyum to have an official state identification card. Hossain thought he could trust Malik, even though he'd just met him, because he had official paperwork showing that he worked for the Department of Motor Vehicles.

Malik said he'd charge seventy-five dollars to walk Kyum through the process of obtaining an identification card. Hossain agreed to pay the fee and provided Malik with documents proving Kyum's identity as well as a bank statement with Kyum's name on it. They agreed that Malik would take Kyum to obtain the identification card and then bring him back to the pizzeria, where Hossain's wife would pay the seventy-five dollars. However, when Malik dropped off Kyum that evening, he handed the new identification card to Hossain's wife but refused to take the money from her for payment. Instead, he asked her to tell Hossain to come to his office in Latham, a suburb fifteen miles north of town, and pay him there.

Upon learning this, Hossain was annoyed. He didn't have the time to drive to Latham to deliver seventy-five dollars. But what Hossain didn't know then was that Malik had a reason for wanting him to come to Latham: he was an FBI informant, and Hossain was his prey.

Malik's real name was Shahed Hussain, and he was many things, in addition to being an FBI informant: an immigrant, a husband, a father, an importer, a convenience store owner, a scam artist, and an accused murderer.

His story begins in Pakistan, and telling it requires a blanket disclaimer: Hussain has exaggerated and lied so often, including under oath in court, that it is difficult to separate truth from invention concerning his biography. As Hussain tells it, he was born into an affluent Karachi family that owned a chain of eateries called Village Restaurants.[2] As a child, he lived next door to the family of Benazir Bhutto, the future prime minister of Pakistan, and grew up enjoying a privileged life, eventually earning a master's in business administration.[3] In the early 1990s, Hussain earned $100,000 per year from his family's chain of six restaurants—a fortune in Pakistan. But after 1992, when the military in Pakistan began to target political opposition parties, Hussain claimed he was victimized, and his family's restaurants were bulldozed.[4] He was also charged with murder, arrested and tortured, and to this day bears a scar on his wrist he claims came from a violent police interrogation.[5] He was released, he said, only after his father bribed the police officers detaining him.[6] How Hussain could simultaneously be friends with Bhutto, then the prime minister, and face such life-threatening political persecution in Pakistan is among the many inconsistencies in a life story the informant has told under oath as a witness for the government.

Reportedly fleeing persecution, Hussain and his family immigrated to the United States in November 1994 with the help of a Russian human smuggler and a few fake British passports. They flew from Karachi to Moscow and then to Mexico City.[7] From there, they drove to the U.S. border and crossed at El Paso, Texas.[8] The human smuggler, however, stayed in the United States only long enough to take back what was his. "The guy that came with us, he took the passport," Hussain explained in court testimony.[9] Hussain and his family, without any kind of documentation, traveled by bus to Albany, where a friend found them an apartment on Central Avenue, not far from the Little Italy Pizzeria.[10] Hussain then applied for, and was granted, political asylum in the United States.[11]

As an immigrant, Hussain was ambitious and entrepreneurial. His first job in Albany was as a gas station attendant earning four dollars per hour.[12] Within seven years, Hussain owned two convenience stores and a middle-class home in a comfortable suburb outside the New York State capital.[13] One of his convenience stores was located next to the Department of Motor Vehicles, and Hussain came to know the employees who stopped in on breaks to buy refreshments and cigarettes. One of those state workers told Hussain about a woman whose business provided translation services to the DMV. Able to speak five languages, Hussain was perfect for that kind of work, which paid well and offered a flexible schedule.

Hussain tppk the job and figured out a way to cheat the system and earn even more money on the side. It started small. DMV test takers would pay him between $300 and $500 to help them cheat on written tests.[14] Since DMV employees didn't speak the languages he was translating the tests into,

Hussain could easily provide the answers or take the tests himself without raising suspicion.[15] If a test taker needed additional assistance, such as passing the road test, Hussain charged a premium and then offered kickbacks to DMV employees who could help with his scam.[16]

In short order, Hussain pulled off his con nearly a hundred times. Then, in December 2001, the FBI sent in an informant who paid Hussain $500 to help him gin up a fake ID.[17] The informant told Hussain he needed a driver's license to become a taxi driver in New York City. "He actually changed the address with the DMV employee and put a false photograph on a license," FBI Special Agent Timothy Coll said of Hussain's handiwork.[18] The FBI arrested Hussain. In addition to as many as one hundred charges in federal court, Hussain faced deportation if convicted. Cutting a deal was the only way he could remain free and in the country, so Hussain agreed to become an FBI informant. At first, he wore a wire and worked against thirteen of his associates in the DMV scam.[19] Some of his targets were friends.[20] He then moved on to narcotics cases in and around Albany. But just as Hussain had been an asset to the DMV for his ability to speak multiple languages, he was a great catch for FBI agents working on national security cases, and the fraudster would soon have his first counterterrorism assignment.

Yassin Aref, a refugee from the Kurdish region of Iraq, arrived in Albany in 1999. The son of an imam, Aref had fled Iraq with his family after the first Gulf War and stayed in Syria before coming to the United States.[21] He initially worked as a janitor at the Albany Medical Center, but after a local university professor donated a building to found a new mosque in town, the Masjid As-Salam, Aref became its imam, earning $18,000 per year.[22]

How the government became interested in Aref isn't clear. What's known is that in late 2002, FBI agents in Albany reported to their counterparts in Atlanta that they had an open investigation of him. In Aref's heavily redacted FBI file, the basis of the government's investigation is not disclosed.[23] However, around the same time that FBI agents in Albany were investigating Aref, U.S. forces in Iraq found a notebook with his name, address, and phone number in it. In front of his name was the Kurdish word *kak*. U.S. authorities initially mistranslated the word to mean *commander*—likely giving them reason to believe Aref was a militant—only to realize much later that *kak* is the word for *brother*, a term of respect. Whatever information the FBI had on Aref, the actions of agents made it clear that the Bureau felt that it needed to draw him out. To do that, the FBI needed to find someone close to the imam.

The candidate for that someone was Mohammed Hossain, who was on the board of directors of Masjid As-Salam. Hussain's showing up at Hossain's pizzeria, giving toy helicopters to his children, and offering to help his brother obtain a state identification card represented the FBI's initial attempts to sidle up to someone close to Aref. That was the reason Hussain didn't collect the money from Hossain's wife when he dropped off Kyum and his new identification card. Hussain and the FBI wanted Hossain to come to a warehouse in Latham—a safe house where hidden cameras could record their conversation.

It was November 20, 2003, a Thursday evening, and Hossain was irritated that he had to drive out to Latham. Thursdays were among the busiest nights of the week at the pizzeria, but since Hussain had helped Kyum obtain an identification card, Hossain felt obligated to go. Just before seven o'clock that evening, after having gotten lost for a short time while searching for the place, Hossain knocked on the warehouse door.

"Where have you been?" Hussain asked in Urdu as he opened the door. Hossain could speak Urdu but was not as confident in the language as he was in his native Bengali.

"That delivery," Hossain answered in Urdu, frustrated. "Today's Thursday. On Thursday there's the delivery."

"So what's the news?" Hussain asked.

Baffled by the question since it was Hussain who had asked him to come to Latham, the pizzeria owner replied with some annoyance: "Nothing. You tell me."

Wearing a white button-down shirt and dress pants, Hussain took a seat behind a small desk. Hossain, wearing a *taqiyah* and a puffy jacket for the cold evening outside, sat in a chair on the other side of the desk.

"Where have you reached in your life?" Hussain asked, attempting small talk.

"There's no praying or meditation or anything," Hossain said.

"Why?"

"So much running around here and there! I'm forced to be so busy with the world's business—there's no worship."

"But we have to do something in this world," Hussain said.

"Well, I just say my prayers," Hossain said.

Hussain then brought up a conversation the two of them had had the last time they'd seen each other, about how serving God and making money weren't mutually exclusive in Islam. "Do you remember the last time when we talked?" Hussain asked. "So I told you that there are two kinds of work to be done in the name of Allah—one is jihad and the other is that one can make money. So what if both are done? So you said that both actions are right. Do you remember?"

"Yes, right, right," Hossain replied.

Hussain went on to explain that he was in the business of importing goods from China, pointing to different areas of the warehouse—a concrete room with bare, white walls and boxes piled in every corner. "All this that you are seeing comes from China, see," he said, adding that among the items he imported were weapons and ammunition. Hussain then stood and pulled back a tarp covering something on the floor. "Do you know what this is?" Hussain asked, his hands on his knees, looking over at his guest. Hossain peered down at the floor, at what had been covered by the tarp. "Do you know what this is?" Hussain asked him again.

"No," he said.

"This is for destroying airplanes," Hussain said, hoisting a device off the floor and placing it on his right shoulder. It was a metal tube, about four feet long, with a shoulder strap hanging from the center. Hussain placed his hand on the front of the tube. "Sensor heat, you know?" he said, holding a shoulder-fired missile he said he had imported from China. "This comes for our *mujahid* brothers," Hussain said. "I have been doing this work for about five years."

"I see."

"This is Muslim work. Understand?"

"Yes, yes."

"For all these Muslim countries. Today it's going to New York. Today it came. This comes in our packaging, in our containers, see."

"I see, I see."

"From China, this will go straight to New York. It will be shipped."

"I see, I see," Hossain said, repeating himself again and showing little interest.

"So, yes, I was thinking I'll show this to my brother as well, that I also do this business for my brothers, my Muslim brothers … This is easily about $4,000, $5,000 worth of merchandise easily."

"Then from New York, it'll be transferred to another place?" Hossain asked.

"I don't have anything to do with that. My job is to get it to New York. You've heard the term 'stinger,' right? This is a SAM, right? This hits planes."

"Yes, yes."

"It's used for hitting the planes. All the *mujahideen* brothers, right?"

"I've seen it on television," Hossain said.

"They use these. This comes from China—it's a Chinese product."

"I had never seen it."

"What?"

"I had never seen it," Hossain said. "I have—but on television."

"On television," Hussain responded. "Did you like this business? So this is one of my other businesses."

"Hmm," Hossain said. "Good money can be made in this?"

"A lot," Hussain interjected.

"But it's not legal," Hossain said.

"What is legal in the world?" Hussain answered, laughing loudly. "There is nothing that is legal in this world—everything has to be illegal. There is a lot of money in this. In this, see, who's going to support our Muslim brothers? People like you, people like me, who have the resources to support, who have the power to support them. Until and unless we support, then we are not Muslims! If you are eating and you don't support your brother, then you are not Muslim."

Hussain kept on talking in this manner. This was one of the informant's regular tactics in the case, talking about things that could be construed as related to terrorism but dominating the conversation to such an extent that Hossain said very little.

Over the next few weeks, Hussain regularly dropped by the Little Italy Pizzeria. He said he admired Hossain's faith, and the two of them often talked about Islam. During those conversations, Hossain mentioned several times that he was short on money. One day, Hussain made him an offer: he'd give him $50,000 in cash, and Hossain could keep $5,000 and pay back the remaining $45,000 in installments over the following year. Hossain agreed, no questions asked. The government would later call this money laundering; Hossain would call it a loan, because his pizza shop was struggling and he needed money to fix up two run-down houses he'd purchased at a city auction. Either way, the transaction would allow the government to inch closer to their target—Yassin Aref, the local imam from Iraq. Hussain and the FBI knew that Hossain would want a religious leader to oversee the financial transaction— a customary request for any devout Muslim—and they also knew how to narrow the candidates down to ensure that the religious leader he chose was Aref.

"I don't want any Pakistani or Bangladeshi or Indian as witness. I don't want these people to know my business," Hussain said when Hossain asked for someone to oversee the transaction.

In Albany, that left only one Muslim as a possible candidate. "How about Brother Yassin as witness?" Hossain asked.

Hussain agreed excitedly. "Holy is Allah," he said.

Hussain arranged to give the first installment of money to Hossain on January 2, 2004. Hussain's FBI handlers told him to make it clear that the money was ill-gotten. "I told him to explain that the money came from—make sure you explain the money came from illegal proceeds," FBI Special Agent Timothy Coll said. "Malik told me the general term used is 'blacken the money,' so I said tell them in your words that the money came from illegal proceeds, that the money is black money, that the money came from under the table, under the tax—to be hidden from taxes."[24] Coll also instructed Hussain to give the money to Hossain and Aref while holding up in plain view the trigger mechanism for a surface-to-air missile.[25] The trigger mechanism is about the size of a large handgun and attaches to the body of the missile launcher. It looks like an oversized label maker when separated from the missile.

Just after two thirty in the afternoon on January 2, Hossain and Aref arrived at the informant's warehouse. They took seats in plastic chairs in front of Hussain's desk. Just as with the previous meeting between Hossain and Hussain, a camera in the corner recorded the conversation. This time, they all spoke in English, since Aref did not speak Urdu.

"Okay, let's do some business, okay? Let's make some money, okay?" Hussain said as he pulled a wad of cash from the desk drawer. "This is $5,000, okay? I want you to count it, okay?"

Hussain handed the money to Aref, who began to count the bills. As he counted, Hussain reached behind and grabbed the trigger mechanism. "When I have to send this in, they will give me $45,000, $50,000, okay?" he said, holding the mechanism aloft. "This is part of the missile that I showed you." Hussain pronounced the word *missile* as *mee-zile*, as if he were attempting a Russian accent. None of this seemed to register with Aref, who never looked up from counting the money. (Aref, whose English is poor, would later maintain he never heard the word *mee-zile* and that he didn't realize the trigger mechanism was part of a weapon.[26]) "So as soon as [the money] comes, I'll give you—this is $5,000, so next couple of weeks, or less, I'll get you more money," Hussain continued.

"*Insha'Allah*," Hossain said. "It's no problem, see, actually, I didn't need all that. I just need to keep going, just so I can pay the bills."[27] Hossain, as the line suggested, believed the money was for a personal loan, not for weapons.

The FBI and Hussain stayed close to Hossain and Aref for the next several months, presumably in the hopes of documenting some type of criminal behavior. There were dozens of conversations during this time, and in some between Hussain and Hossain, the informant used a code word for the missile, *chaudry*. According to the government, this was evidence that Hossain knew about the missile, but from the transcripts, it isn't clear whether Hossain knew the informant's meaning of *chaudry*. Hossain also began to pay back Hussain with regular checks, as he had agreed, suggesting that the pizzeria owner truly believed their arrangement constituted a loan, not money laundering. In fact, on the memo line of one check, he wrote that it was for a loan repayment.

Finally, after seven months without criminal activity by either Hossain or Aref, the FBI arrested the pair in August 2004, charging them with conspiring to aid a terrorist group, providing support for a weapon of mass destruction, money laundering, and supporting a foreign terrorist organization. They went to trial together in September and October 2006.

Because Hossain and Aref had not encountered a real terrorist during the entire FBI operation—only an informant posing as an arms importer for terrorists—the prosecution needed to find a way to link Hossain's and Aref's recorded statements to terrorism. For that, the U.S. government turned to Evan Kohlmann, a then-twenty-seven-year-old self-described terrorism expert whom an FBI agent once dubbed "the Doogie Howser of terrorism."

A Florida native whose Manhattan apartment walls are covered with pictures of terrorists, Kohlmann is the government's most prolific terrorism expert, having served as an expert witness in seventeen terrorism trials in the United States and in nine others abroad since 2002. With most of his knowledge gleaned from the Internet—the type of information the CIA describes as "open source intelligence"—Kohlmann has testified to juries about the history of Islamic terrorism, how terrorist organizations finance themselves, and how they spread propaganda and recruit others for terrorist acts. Since 9/11, Kohlmann has made a living testifying for the prosecution in terrorism trials as well as appearing on cable news as a terrorism expert. Jonathan Turley, a constitutional law professor at George Washington University, described Kohlmann to New York magazine as having been "grown hydroponically in the basement of the Bush Justice Department."[28] Several defense lawyers, including those in the cases of "dirty bomber" Jośe Padilla and the so-called Virginia jihad group, have tried to have Kohlmann disqualified as an expert witness, arguing that his only qualifications as a terrorism expert are self-fashioned.[29] However, because few experts with university credentials and social science backgrounds are willing to testify about terrorism, the Justice Department has had little trouble persuading judges to allow Kohlmann to take the stand, where, as one of his critics put it, he spews "junk science" by suggesting that anyone who watches jihadi videos has self-radicalized.[30]

Kohlmann is one of a cadre of self-appointed terrorism experts who today earn handsome paychecks pushing forward the idea that Islamic terrorism is a real and immediate threat in the United States. Among Kohlmann's peers is Rita Katz, an Iraqi-born Jewish woman who has helped the U.S. government investigate Islamic charities and mosques linked to radicals. One of Katz's critics alleged that, like Kohlmann, she could find a way to trace just about anything to Islamic terrorism, telling the *Boston Globe* that she "fits everything into a mold—that there is a Muslim terrorist under everybody's bed."[31] Many of these so-called terrorism experts, including Kohlmann and Katz, have worked under Steven Emerson, a former journalist who has earned millions of dollars while making such hyperbolic claims as that 80 percent of mosques in the United States are controlled by Islamic extremists. In 2009 and 2010, Emerson's nonprofit organization, Investigative Project on Terrorism Foundation, raised $5.4 million in grants and individual contributions.[32] The nonprofit then paid Emerson's corporation, SAE Productions, $3.4 million in management fees, allowing the tax-exempt Investigative Project on Terrorism Foundation to act as a pass-through for a for-profit company—a questionable but not illegal practice. Simply put, there's a lot of money to be made in stoking terrorism fears. For testifying in the trial of Hossain and Aref, for example, the U.S. government paid Evan Kohlmann $5,000.

To establish a terrorist connection, the prosecution played a conversation the FBI had recorded between Hossain and Hussain. "We are members of Jamaat-e-Islami," Hossain told Hussain in the recording. The government had originally claimed that Jamaat-e-Islami, a political party in Bangladesh, was linked to terrorism through a proxy organization, Jamaat-ul-Mujahideen. But when Kohlmann was named an expert witness in the case, replacing another government expert who was unable to testify at the trial, he submitted a report that seemed to confuse Jamaat-e-Islami of Pakistan with Jamaat-e-Islami of Bangladesh—two different organizations. In a deposition, Kevin A. Luibrand, a lawyer for Hossain, challenged not only Kohlmann's assertion, but also his general political knowledge of Bangladesh. Under questioning, Kohlmann admitted that he had never written about Jamaat-e-Islami of Bangladesh and could not say how many political parties existed in Bangladesh or even who the current prime minister of the country was.

"Can you name any of the major political parties in Bangladesh from the year 2000 to 2004?" Luibrand asked.

"Other than Jamaat-e-Islami?"

"Yes."

"That's—I'm not familiar off the top of my head," Kohlmann said.

"Have you ever heard of an organization known as the Bangladesh National Party?"

"Vaguely."

"Do you know what it is?"

"I'm assuming it's a political party, but again—the name vaguely sounds familiar but—"

"Do you know what, if anything, it stands for politically within Bangladesh?"

"Sorry, can't tell ya."

"You can't tell me because you don't know?"

"I don't know off the top of my head."

Following this exchange, Luibrand petitioned the court

to have Kohlmann disqualified as an expert witness, writing in his motion: "Evan Kohlmann revealed that he has no basis to form any opinions with respect to JEI Bangladesh, or to explain JEI Bangladesh to the jury."[33] The presiding judge denied the request, and Kohlmann was allowed to testify not only about Jamaat-e-Islami but also about Ansar al Islam, a terrorist group formed by a man Yassin Aref had met a few times while living as a refugee in Syria. Of the damage Kohlmann's testimony did at trial, Hossain's lawyer said it "just kill[ed] us."[34]

A jury ultimately found Hossain and Aref guilty of money laundering—but not of the more significant terrorism charges. At sentencing, both men were mystified about how they'd arrived in the position they were in—as accused terrorists about to be sentenced to federal prison.

"I never had any intention to harm anyone in this country," Aref told the judge. "And I don't know why I'm guilty."

"I am just a pizza man," Hossain said. "I make good pizza."

The public in Albany was largely supportive of Hossain and Aref, believing an injustice had occurred. Community members pressed into the courtroom, some holding copies of Aref's self-published autobiography, *Son of Mountains*. Fred LeBrun, the metro columnist for the *Albany Times Union*, compared the prosecution to U.S. Senator Joseph McCarthy's witch hunts and the internment of Japanese-Americans during World War II. But U.S. District Judge Thomas McAvoy, indifferent to the community support, sentenced the pair to fifteen years in prison.

Yassin Aref is incarcerated in a special Indiana prison that restricts outside communication. The ACLU is representing him in challenging his confinement there. If Aref's counterpart, Mohammed Hossain, were ever a terrorist threat, you wouldn't know it today based on his assignment at the U.S. Bureau of Prisons: he is serving his sentence at Schuylkill Federal Correctional Institute, a medium-security facility located in a poor, rural part of Pennsylvania, between Allentown and Harrisburg.

The day I visited Hossain in March 2012, he was wearing a prison-issued, button-down blue shirt with gray pants. His name and prisoner number were embroidered on the left side of the shirt. Less than halfway through his sentence, he didn't have a lot of hope of being released early. His initial appeal had been denied, and he was now drafting a second appeal himself, enlisting other inmates to help him with the spelling and grammar.

We sat across from each other on plastic chairs in an empty concrete room. Toys filled a small adjacent room, for when inmates receive their families. A bank of vending machines lined one of the walls. Three guards stood in the corner talking about baseball. From having researched Hossain's case, I knew that Hussain, the informant, was a bad actor—a scam artist and an aggressive prevaricator who was, as FBI Special Agent Timothy Coll put it so well, "good at being deceptive."[35] But I found it hard to reason away Hossain's inaction during the sting operation. For example, on November 20, 2003, when Hossain came to Hussain's warehouse to drop off the seventy-five dollars for his brother Kyum's state identification card, the FBI informant showed him the shoulder-fired missile and said in Urdu, "This is for destroying airplanes." Hossain didn't leave and report the missile to authorities. He just sat there, and then replied with a statement most Americans would think incriminating: "Holy is Allah." I also could not understand why, even if

Hossain thought the money the informant gave him was for a loan, he'd accept cash from a man he'd seen shouldering a missile as he bragged about knowing mujahideen.

Stroking his beard, which is long and gray and hangs down to his waist, Hossain tried to explain himself. "You have to understand," Hossain told me. "He hounded me. Everywhere I went, he was there." From the day Hussain gave the toy helicopters to Hossain's children in front of the Little Italy Pizzeria, he said, the informant became a fixture in his life. Hussain said he wanted to become a better Muslim and admired Hossain for his faith. Despite being busy, Hossain said he felt a religious obligation to talk to Hussain about Islam. He'd walk into the pizza shop's kitchen, and Hussain would follow him, asking questions. "I told him once I have to go deliver pizzas, and he said, 'No problem, I'll come with you.'"

During their conversations, Hussain would often talk about himself, describing how he ran an import business bringing in goods from China—the kind of cheap and small items you find in dollar stores—and bragging about having a relationship with the FBI. Once, when Hossain described some problems he was having with a tenant, Hussain offered to call his FBI friend and ask if he could assist. Hossain demurred. He had no reason to suspect Hussain was anything but a legitimate businessman with influential friends in law enforcement. That's what he said he was thinking when Hussain pulled back the tarp at the warehouse and lifted a missile launcher to his shoulder.

"It looked like a telescope or some plumbing equipment," Hossain told me. "Then he said it was a missile. You have to understand what I was thinking. Do you remember when Iraq was at war with Iran? Who did America back? Iraq. They sent weapons to Iraq. In Afghanistan, America gave weapons to the mujahideen to fight the Soviets. He said he had licenses to import from China and that he knew an FBI agent. I believed it was a legitimate business, that what he was doing was legal. I couldn't prove it wasn't legal. I ran a pizza shop, and every day, I would make sure the floors were clean and dry, and if they were slippery, I'd put up a sign. I knew that if I didn't and someone fell, they'd sue me. They'd hurt me and my family. So what if I went to the police and told them about Malik and the missile? I thought he could sue me for a false report, and he would take all my money and all my properties." Hossain added that Hussain came to the pizza shop the day after showing him the missile and assured him that everything was legal and on the up and up.

At one point, the FBI informant asked Hossain if he'd be interested in donating money to a school in Pakistan. "I told him that even if I had money, I wouldn't be interested," Hossain said. "But I also told him that I didn't have money then. I told him that I purchased two homes from the city auction, and I needed $3,000 to $4,000 to buy new boilers." Hussain said he could help and offered to loan him $50,000. "I didn't need his money. I could have gotten the money from other people," Hossain told me. "But I wanted him to go away. I thought if I agreed to do something with him, he'd leave me alone. People are like that—they bother you until you do what they want and then they leave. I thought that would happen." As a result, Hossain agreed to accept the loan, and to this day maintains that he did not know that what he was doing could be considered money laundering or that the money was supposed to have come from a terrorist organization. "Why would I be a terrorist? I had a family, a business, nearly $1 million in properties," Hossain said. "If someone did a terrorist attack in Albany, it would have hurt me just like everyone else. My family would have been in danger. My business would have been hurt. I have never had anything to do with terrorism."

Hossain suffers from diabetes and hypertension, and incarceration has been hard for him. But it's been even harder for his family, he said. He was the sole breadwinner, and in the wake of his trial and incarceration, he and his family lost the pizza shop. But he lost much more in the following years. "Children need a father. My children, they are lost to the world now," he said.

I asked him what he meant by that.

"They fall into the wrong crowd," he said. "I do not know them anymore."

He then pointed to the appeal he is drafting—a thick stack of paper with amateur copyediting notes on the pages correcting typos and grammatical errors. The appeal described the FBI informant's aggressive behavior and particular instances in which Hossain alleged his Urdu statements were mistranslated to sound more incriminating than they actually were. He has already lost one appeal that his lawyers filed, so this jailhouse petition doesn't offer him much promise. But it's all he has now—a final effort to reverse a decision by a jury he believes was overwhelmed by the government's claims and biased by his appearance.

"Look at me," Hossain said. "My beard, my face, my taqiyah—I look like Osama bin Laden."

Hossain paused.

"I hate Osama bin Laden."

Since 9/11, Shahed Hussain and informants like him have become one of the Bureau's most valuable commodities in the war on terrorism—aggressive men indentured to the FBI who are willing to do anything to take down their targets and who also have the ability to "play the part" of terrorists in front of hidden cameras and microphones. This ability to betray others for personal gain, however, reveals a dark aspect to the FBI's use of informants; namely, that the best informants are also those who tend toward criminal behavior themselves. Hussain is a classic example of this. While working for the FBI, he filed for Chapter 13 bankruptcy protection in 2003, claiming $145,075 in personal assets, including his $125,000 home, and reporting $177,766.72 in debts. According to the filing, Hussain owed, among other debts, $18,377.72 to the Albany County Treasurer and $30,000 to HSBC Bank. Through the bankruptcy court, Hussain delayed payment to his creditors and negotiated lower settlement amounts for some of the debts.

But the FBI informant never told the bankruptcy court about some substantial assets he had, including an expensive Mercedes he said his family had been given by an old friend, former Pakistani prime minister Benazir Bhutto, and $500,000 in a trust fund in Pakistan.[36] While in bankruptcy reorganization, Hussain transferred the money from Pakistan to the United States and, in an apparent effort to hide his connection to the money, deposited the cash in a bank account in his son's name.[37] Hussain then used some of that money to purchase and fix up a run-down hotel near Saratoga Springs, New York. He listed the hotel—originally called the Hideaway Motel but renamed the Crest Inn Suites and Cottages—in his wife's name.[38] Hussain's actions as a hotelier were reportedly as dishonest as his dealings as an FBI snitch, as three would-be guests sued him for fraudulent misrepresentation after they prepaid for hotel rooms that were not available upon arrival.[39] In addition, the reviews the hotel has received on TripAdvisor are poor, with two guests claiming to have been cheated while staying there.

But none of this crooked activity seemed to matter to the FBI, which made Hussain a paid informant after the Aref case. In all, Hussain spent four and a half years serving FBI agents in and around Albany, receiving $60,000 in expenses and working off his criminal charges related to the DMV scam. Staying on with the Bureau was Hussain's preference, as well. "I liked to work with the FBI," he said.[40]

In 2007, FBI agents in Albany called their counterparts in White Plains, New York, and offered them the use of Hussain as an informant. FBI Special Agent Robert Fuller, who was involved in the extraordinary rendition of Maher Arar, a dual Canadian Syrian citizen detained at John F. Kennedy International Airport and then deported to Syria and tortured, accepted the offer.[41] He sent Hussain to Pakistan to investigate a possible terrorist camp and then to London to check out a mosque that was allegedly raising money for Palestinians in Gaza. Each time Hussain returned to the United States, Fuller met him at Kennedy Airport to make sure immigration officials allowed him back into the country. As we saw in the case of Foad Farahi, the FBI often uses shaky immigration status as a means of keeping informants, even paid ones, on a leash.

Despite his international travels, Hussain's most ambitious assignment under Fuller would come closer to home. In September 2007, the informant began praying regularly in Newburgh, a struggling former Air Force town with few decent jobs about an hour north of New York City. It was a fishing expedition. "I was not looking for targets," Hussain said in court testimony. "I was finding people who would be harmful, who can do harm, and radicals, and identify them for the FBI."[42] As in the Albany case, Hussain's cover story was that he imported goods from China, and Fuller instructed him to tell people that he was an agent for the Pakistani terrorist group Jaish-e-Mohammed. Most of Newburgh's Muslim residents were poor, and Hussain, who posed as a wealthy businessman and wore expensive clothing and drove high-end cars, easily made plenty of friends. But after more than a year of trawling the local Muslim community, he had not identified a single target.[43]

Then he met James Cromitie, a forty-five-year-old stocker at the local Walmart. A former drug addict with a history of mental instability—he once admitted to a psychiatrist that he heard and saw things that weren't there—Cromitie had adopted the name Abdul Rahman after converting to Islam while serving two years in prison for selling crack cocaine in 1987.[44] However, by 2008, he had seemingly turned his life around. He had a job, a girlfriend, and a room he rented, and he prayed regularly at Masjid Al-Ikhlas, a large, tan-colored mosque. Below the surface, though, Cromitie was an angry, bigoted man, believing others discriminated against him because of his religion, and openly hating Jews.

In June 2008, Cromitie met a man from Pakistan at Masjid Al-Ikhlas who said his name was Maqsood. Everyone at the mosque had seen or knew of Maqsood. It was impossible not to know about him, because in poor Newburgh, Maqsood made an impression. He was always driving one of four expensive cars—a Hummer, a Mercedes or one of two different BMWs—and had been coming to the mosque so frequently that he had been invited to become a board member.[44] Of course, the man's name wasn't really Maqsood—it was Shahed Hussain.

It was in the parking lot of Masjid Al-Ikhlas that Cromitie first approached Hussain. The two men began talking, and Hussain told Cromitie that he was destined for much more in this life. "Allah didn't bring you here to work for Walmart," he said.[46] What exactly happened between the pair in the weeks following that initial encounter in the parking lot isn't known, because from June to October 2008, Special Agent Fuller chose not to have Hussain record these conversations. But whatever happened and whatever was said, it allowed Hussain and Cromitie to become close.

By the time the FBI began recording their conversations on October 12, 2008, Hussain was already an experienced hand at fueling Cromitie's bigotry and bolstering his personal narrative of persecution as a misunderstood Muslim.

"A lot of Jews up here. They look at me like they would like to kill me when they see me inside my jalabiya, everything they say. I don't salaam them either," Cromitie told Hussain.

"Does that make you angry, brother?" Hussain asked, clearly knowing the answer he was soliciting.

"It doesn't make me angry. It just make [sic] me want to jump up and kill one of them," Cromitie said.

"Wow," Hussain replied.

Cromitie then talked about the Jews he met while working at Walmart. They looked at him strangely, he said, and the Jewish women refused to allow him to carry their bags to the car.

During the course of their conversations, Hussain would seize on any opportunity to amplify Cromitie's paranoia and hatred of Jews. "I was reading in one of the newspapers, in the *New York Times*, that every second advisor in the White House, they *yahuds*," Hussain told Cromitie during one meeting.[47]

"Every who?" Cromitie asked.

"Every second advisor to the president is a yahud," Hussain repeated.

"In the White House?"

"Yeah," Hussain said.

"The worst brother in the whole Islamic world is better than 10 billion yahudi," Cromitie answered.

Hussain told Cromitie that if he was angry for the way the world was, he could change it. But he needed to change it through jihad. "I always think about going for a cause, you know? For a cause of Islam. Have you ever thought about that, brother?" Hussain asked.

"Have I ever thought about going for the cause?" Cromitie asked.

"Cause of Islam," Hussain clarified.

In November 2008, Hussain invited Cromitie to attend the Muslim Alliance in North America conference in Philadelphia. The local imam from Masjid Al-Ikhlas would be there, as would one of Cromitie's idols, Imam Siraj Wahhaj, an African American convert to Islam whose mosque is in Brooklyn. Hussain offered to cover all of Cromitie's expenses, which of course were covered by the FBI. By this time, Hussain had told Cromitie about his import business and said he could bring in weapons and missiles from China. Not to be outdone by Hussain's peacocking, Cromitie portrayed himself in conversations with the informant as something of a badass, claiming to have firebombed a police precinct, to have a brother who stole $126 million in merchandise from Tiffany & Co., to have formed a small militia, and to have stolen guns from Walmart.[48] These claims were all untrue. Whether the FBI knew at the time that Cromitie was nothing but talk is unclear, but the conference in Philadelphia would prove to be a turning point for Hussain and the Bureau.

It was late at night on Friday, November 28, 2008, and Hussain and Cromitie were driving to Philadelphia in the FBI informant's Hummer. The vehicle had been wired for sound, and all of their conversations during the nearly four-hour trip were recorded. About halfway through the drive Cromitie went silent.

"What are you thinking, brother?" Hussain asked.

"I'm just thinking that I'm gonna try to put a plan together. What type of plan? I don't know yet. I'm gonna put a good plan together," Cromitie answered.

"May Allah be with you and Allah find you the way," Hussain said.

The next day, Hussain and Cromitie attended the conference in Philadelphia, where they saw the imam from Newburgh and listened to an inflammatory speech Siraj Wahhaj gave during a dinner. In their private conversations, Hussain kept asking about a security group Cromitie claimed to have formed to protect Newburgh-area Muslims—Cromitie called the group his "sutra team"—and what type of actions they had done in the past.

"We couldn't get hold of a bomb like we wanted to, but we was doing all type of stuff," Cromitie said. "You probably heard. We was blowing police cars up. We was throwing gas bombs inside." Cromitie was lying about all of it, of course. But he did know a few thugs-for-hire, Newburgh men who he said would be willing to join an attack for the right price. "They would do it for the money," Cromitie told Hussain. "They're not even thinking about the cause."

Later that same day, Hussain asked Cromitie what

he thought would be the best target for a terrorist attack. Cromitie's response was a bridge. "But bridges are too hard to be hit, because of they're, they're made of steel," Hussain told him.

"Of course they're made of steel," Cromitie said. "But the same way they can be put up, they can be brought down."

If Hussain and the FBI were going to bring Cromitie into a terrorist plot, they needed to guide him toward a more manageable idea than bombing a bridge. A few days before the Philadelphia conference, the Pakistani terrorist group Lashkar-e-Taiba had killed 364 people in a coordinated attack in Mumbai, India, that targeted hotels, a café, a railway station, and a Jewish community center. Special Agent Fuller instructed Hussain to bring up the Mumbai attacks, which he believed would help dissuade Cromitie from his ambition to bomb a bridge.

"Eight spots were hit at the same time," Hussain told Cromitie, referring to the terrorist attack in India.

"Yeah, yeah, eight, I saw it," Cromitie replied.

"You saw it. The railroad station. Hotels, the Jews—"

"Yeah," Cromitie interrupted.

"The Jew center, the main Jew center," Hussain continued.

"Yahudi," Cromitie said.

"Yahudi center. Uh, the cafés where the Americans, and there's this, uh—"

"That too," Cromitie interjected. "The cafés and shit like that. Sometime the biggest people be in these places and you don't know, but shit happens. You understand?"

After a few more minutes of talking, Hussain pressed Cromitie to move forward. "Do you think you are a better recruiter or a better action man? I'm asking you a question on it," Hussain said.[49]

"I'm both," Cromitie bragged.

"My people would be very happy to know that, brother. Honestly," Hussain said.

"Who's your people?" Cromitie asked.

"Jaish-e-Mohammed."

That answer was supposed to make it clear that Hussain was a well-connected terrorist. But Cromitie had never heard of Jaish-e-Mohammed, which is among the world's better-known Islamic terrorist organizations. "Who are they?" he asked. "What are, what are your people? What are they, Muslim?"

"What do you think?" Hussain asked.

"What are they, Muslim?" Cromitie repeated.

"What do you think we are?"

Cromitie had no clue. However, the fact that Cromitie had never heard of the terrorist organization the FBI was using for its cover was not enough to stop the Bureau from pushing forward with a sting built around a luckless man they inexplicably viewed as a would-be terrorist.

After they returned from Philadelphia, Hussain and Cromitie discussed their proposed attack, with Hussain suggesting they target nearby Stewart International Airport, which includes an Air National Guard base, as well as a few synagogues. But after deciding on the specifics of their plot, Hussain had to leave the area for nearly two months—he told Cromitie he had to go to New York City to meet with other members of Jaish-e-Mohammed—and he asked Cromitie to spend their time apart recruiting people and doing reconnaissance on the targets for the attack.

However, without the informant driving the action in Newburgh, the plot ran aground. While Hussain was gone,

Cromitie spent his time working at Walmart, hanging around Newburgh, and watching a lot of television—mostly, in a wonderful irony, Hollywood action movies involving Islamic terrorists. When Hussain finally returned on February 23, 2009, Cromitie had accomplished nothing. "I been watching a lot of crazy pictures lately," Cromitie told Hussain, as if to explain his inaction. "Well, terrorist movies. A whole bunch of them. And America makes these movies. That's the shit that kill [*sic*] me. And then I look at all of these movies, and I say to myself, 'Why is America trying to make the Arab brothers look like they the bad guys?'"

The sting was going nowhere, and Hussain needed to get it back on track. He told Cromitie that Jaish-e-Mohammed was very happy with him, and that his superiors had given him authorization to carry out the attack with Cromitie and any men he could recruit. Hussain said the attack would teach people a lesson—but Cromitie was just as clueless as before about what they were doing, for whom, and why.

"Who are we teaching a lesson to?" he asked.

"The people who are killing innocent Muslims," Hussain answered.

With the FBI informant back in Newburgh to provoke the action, the plan became serious again. Hussain and Cromitie came up with code words—guns were *mangoes*, missiles *noodles*, phones *eggs*—and Hussain asked Cromitie to go with him to collect information about target sites. "Let's speed up the process," Hussain said, a reference to how Cromitie had accomplished so little while he was away.

With Hussain's encouragement, Cromitie recruited three members of his so-called sutra team. They were all small-time thugs and converts to Islam. David Williams was a twenty-eight-year-old who went by the name Daoud. He had spent time in prison for drugs and weapons possession charges and had been released from parole supervision in May 2008. Onta Williams (no relation to David Williams) was a thirty-two-year-old high school dropout who went by the name Hamza and had done three months in jail on a drug charge. Laguerre Payen, a twenty-seven-year-old who went by the name Amin, had served one year in prison for an assault charge for shooting two sixteen-year-olds in the head and eye with a BB gun.

With three recruits now on board and targets selected, the FBI still wasn't convinced the sting would work. If Cromitie backed out of the plot, the whole operation would fall apart. So Special Agent Fuller instructed Hussain to give Cromitie $1,800 and ask him to buy some guns. If the sting operation imploded, the FBI would at least have weapons charges to bring against Cromitie.

Even as a goon, though, Cromitie was hopeless. He couldn't find anyone to sell him a gun, resorting at one point to throwing stones at a drug dealer's second-story window in the hopes of waking him and asking if he had any firearms to sell. But the drug dealer wasn't home, and in the end, Cromitie returned the money to Hussain. The target of a months-long FBI terrorism sting wasn't even capable of obtaining a Saturday Night Special with $1,800 in his pocket.

With the sting now progressing in waves, a flurry of action pushed by Hussain followed by long periods of inaction, it was becoming clear that Cromitie wasn't the die-hard jihadi the U.S. government would ultimately portray him as to the news media. Within weeks of Hussain's return to Newburgh, for example, Cromitie traveled to North Carolina to pick up extra work stocking a new Walmart location. He then went several weeks without even talking to Hussain until calling him on April 5, 2009. By that time, the FBI informant had left Newburgh for New Jersey.

"I have to try to make some money, brother," Cromitie told Hussain, explaining why he had gone to North Carolina.

"I told you I can make you $250,000, but you don't want it, brother," Hussain said. "What can I tell you?"

"Okay, come see me, brother. Come see me."

How much Cromitie, in finally moving forward in the plot with Hussain, was acting out of ideological commitment or financial interest is questionable. Hussain would later admit at trial that he created the—in his word—"impression" that Cromitie would make a lot of money by participating in the bombing plot.[50] When asked about the phone conversation in which he offered Cromitie $250,000, Hussain said the phrase "$250,000" was simply code for the plot—code, he admitted, that only he knew.[51]

This also wasn't the only time Hussain used financial inducements when Cromitie was reluctant to become a terrorist. At various times during the sting operation, Hussain gave Cromitie money to pay his rent—money that had come from the FBI.[52] He also at one point offered to buy him a barbershop.[53] "What will it cost—$60,000, $70,000 to build it?" Hussain asked.[54] Indeed, Cromitie and the three men he recruited all ultimately believed there would be a financial reward for participating in the terrorist plot, which had now evolved into a plan to plant bombs inside parked cars in front of synagogues in the Bronx and then return to Newburgh, where they'd fire Stinger missiles at planes. Hussain told Cromitie his organization could provide everything they'd need—the transportation, the bombs, the missiles.

On April 7, 2009, at two forty-five in the afternoon, Cromitie went to Hussain's home on Shipp Street in Newburgh—

which was an FBI safe house.[55] A hidden camera recorded everything that happened in the living room, and FBI agents in a van around the corner watched the action live. It took this meeting for Hussain to make Cromitie comfortable with the prospect that their attack would kill and maim, but to do so, he had to fuel once again Cromitie's hatred of the U.S. military and Jews.

"I don't want anyone to get hurt," Cromitie told Hussain. "You understand what I'm saying?"

"If there is American soldiers, I don't care," Hussain said, egging on Cromitie.

"Hold up," he answered. "If it's American soldiers, I don't even care."

"If it's kids, I care," Hussain said. "If it's women, I care."

"I care. That's what I'm worried about. And I'm going to tell you, I don't care if it's a whole synagogue of men."

"Yep."

"I would take 'em down, I don't even care. 'Cause I know they are the ones."

"We have the equipment to do it," Hussain said.

"See, see, I'm not worried about nothing. Ya know? What I'm worried about is my safety," Cromitie said.

"Oh, yeah, safety comes first."

"I want to get in and I want to get out."

"Trust me," Hussain assured.[56]

Three days later, Hussain, Cromitie, and David Williams went to Walmart and purchased a digital camera, which they used to take photographs of Stewart International Airport and synagogues in Riverdale, a heavily Jewish area of the Bronx.

On April 23, 2009, Cromitie returned to the Shipp Street house, this time with David Williams. On the living room coffee table was a bomb—the type they would place in parked cars in front of the synagogues. Cromitie stared at the weapon. "What's the distance?" he asked Hussain.[57]

"It's, like, a hundred, hundred miles' range," Hussain answered. "So, it's with a cell phone, so if you put it up there, you come out back here. You can sit down here, and it blows up."

Cromitie laughed and fist-bumped David Williams.

The next day, Hussain, Cromitie, and David Williams drove to the airport to scout for an ideal area from which to fire the Stinger missiles. They purchased four cell phones for use during the attack, and all four men—Cromitie, David Williams, Onta Williams, and Laguerre Payen—then met Hussain at a storage facility in Newburgh, where the FBI informant showed them the C-4 explosives to be used and demonstrated how to operate the Stinger missile system. They set a date for the attack: May 20, 2009.

By this time, it was clear that none of the men was doing the attack for ideological reasons; they were doing it for cash. How much money they believed they were doing it for remains a mystery; officially, the FBI authorized Hussain to offer $5,000 to each man. The night before the attack, the informant took the four men to a T.G.I. Friday's for dinner—"a last supper," as Hussain called it. Over dinner they purportedly discussed money. But the FBI did not record the meeting. Special Agent Fuller gave Hussain his instructions, as he always did before meetings with Cromitie and his group, but unlike for the dozens of earlier meetings, the agent didn't give the informant a recording device. Whatever Hussain said over the meal, it was enough to ensure that Cromitie and his three associates carried forward with the plot.

On the evening of May 20, 2009, the four men piled into Hussain's car and headed south toward New York

City. Though Hussain had previously shown Cromitie how to activate the bombs—which were, in fact, inert—Cromitie couldn't figure out how to activate them himself once they were on the road. Hussain, who was driving, had to pull over and activate the bombs from the side of the highway. Upon their arrival in the Bronx, the four men got out of the car while Hussain stayed behind the wheel. Cromitie wanted to deliver the bombs himself, and he asked David Williams, Onta Williams, and Laguerre Payen to serve as lookouts. Hussain was to remain in the car as the getaway driver.

As the informant promised, there were three cars parked in front of the Riverdale Temple and Riverdale Jewish Center, which are located less than a quarter of a mile from each other on Independence Avenue. Cromitie placed a bomb in the trunks of each of the cars as instructed and then ran to the getaway car. While he believed he was placing deadly and destructive bombs in cars parked there by other Jaish-e-Mohammed operatives, in reality he was putting props into the trunks of rental cars that had been parked there by FBI agents.

Cromitie opened the door to Hussain's car and climbed into the passenger seat. Just then, a SWAT team consisting of local and federal law enforcement officers surrounded the car and shattered the windows. Glass rained in as Hussain lifted his hands to shield his face. The FBI informant then looked down; his hands were bleeding from the broken glass. But Hussain's job was done. He would receive $96,000 for his work in the case.[58]

The FBI charged James Cromitie, David Williams, Onta Williams, and Laguerre Payen—whom the media would dub the Newburgh Four—with conspiracy to use a weapon of mass destruction, attempted use of weapons of mass destruction, conspiracy to acquire and use anti-aircraft missiles, and conspiracy to kill officers of the United States.

The Bureau held a news conference following the arrests.

"Did you believe they were a genuine threat?" a reporter asked Joseph Demarest, the head of the FBI's New York office.

"Yes, based on what they intended to do and based on their actions," Demarest said. "They planted the satchels, or bags, with what they believed to contain explosives, in front of two Jewish temples."

"Did they have any experience in knowing if what they had was real?" the reporter followed.

"No, not that we're aware of," Demarest answered.[59]

The four men pleaded not guilty to the charges, and their defense lawyers attempted to show at trial that Shahed Hussain had baited the desperate and susceptible men with money and lies. But the jury was unsympathetic to the argument and found all four guilty following a one-month trial.

At James Cromitie's sentencing hearing, U.S. District Judge Colleen McMahon appeared to agree with many of the arguments the Newburgh Four's lawyers had made. "The essence of what occurred here is that a government, understandably zealous to protect its citizens from terrorism, came upon a man both bigoted and suggestible, one who was incapable of committing an act of terrorism on his own," McMahon said. "It created acts of terrorism out of his fantasies of bravado and bigotry, and then made those fantasies come true . . . . I suspect that real terrorists would not have bothered themselves with a person who was so utterly inept." McMahon continued, "Only the government could have made a terrorist out of Mr. Cromitie, whose buffoonery is positively Shakespearean in scope." The judge then sentenced each of the four men to twenty-five years in prison, the minimum sentence available to her under federal sentencing guidelines.

At the same hearing, Cromitie told Judge McMahon: "I am not a violent person. I've never been a terrorist, and I never will be. I got myself into this stupid mess. I know I said a lot of stupid stuff."[60]

With the convictions of the Newburgh Four, Shahed Hussain was now an all-star FBI informant, having been at the center of two successful terrorism stings. FBI agents told me that even after the Newburgh trial, during which defense lawyers provided evidence showing that Hussain had lied or withheld information from criminal and bankruptcy courts, Hussain continued to be used as an informant and was considered among the Bureau's top terrorism snitches. Hussain liked working for the FBI—he said so himself during court testimony—but what makes his work as an informant so troubling is that he, like other snitches, was motivated purely by self-interest.

In addition to payments during the course of an investigation, informants receive what the FBI terms "performance incentives" when sting operations result in convictions. The amounts of these payments are never disclosed, though one former agent told me that six-figure paydays are not unusual for high-profile cases. Performance incentives serve two purposes for the FBI. The first, and most obvious, is that they keep informants hungry; they know that if they can bring home a conviction with their testimony, they'll be in line for a handsome payday. But the second, and more important, reason for withholding an informant's full payment until after conviction has to do with the fear of coloring a jury's opinion. A paid informant is always a problem for prosecutors, as defense lawyers will use the payments to suggest that the informant has motivation to lie on the witness stand because the government is paying him. The more he's paid, the more motivation he has to deceive, the logic goes. For that reason, the fact that Hussain received $96,000 for his work during the Newburgh Four investigation presented a challenge for prosecutors, since defense lawyers during the trial made references to the payments in clear attempts to bias the jury against the FBI's informant. What the jury never learned, however, was that Hussain would receive even more money if Cromitie and his three co-defendants were convicted. Even Hussain himself didn't know exactly how much money he'd receive, as FBI agents never tell informants the amount of their performance incentive and never guarantee that they will receive a performance incentive at all, since not knowing this information safeguards informants from having to testify about it at trial, which would give defense lawyers even more fodder to use when trying to undermine the informant's credibility. "They have an expectation that there's a performance incentive waiting for them at the end of the trial," an FBI agent told me, asking that his name not be used because he was not authorized to talk about the subject. "But all we tell them is, 'Hey, we'll take care of you at the end of it.'"

Because payments to informants come out only at trial, and the trial is over by the time the FBI pays performance incentives, the amount of incentive money Hussain received after the Newburgh Four trial has never been revealed and is exempted from disclosure under the Freedom of Information Act. But it's safe to assume that the payment was substantial, since Hussain continues to work for the FBI. In fact, the money paid to informants such as Hussain underpins a fundamental injustice present in all informant-led terrorism sting operations: that it's against the financial interest of informants not to help make people into terrorists. That's why FBI informants are so aggressive in pushing forward terrorist plots. Finding terrorists, even ones led by the nose into plots, pays substantial dividends.

In the months after the trial of the Newburgh Four, I made several attempts to meet with Shahed Hussain. However, he never responded to any of the messages I left or the letters I sent. In February 2011, I drove to the Crest Inn Suites and Cottages, the hotel he'd purchased with some of the hundreds of thousands of dollars he had stashed away in an account in Pakistan. The hotel is about forty-five minutes north of Albany. A storm had come through New York two days before I arrived, and the snowbanks along the roads were piled several feet high.

Hussain's hotel was dumpy and in the middle of nowhere, the only nearby attraction the horse racing track in Saratoga Springs. The green and yellow sign had been freshly painted. A Mercedes Benz and a BMW were parked outside near the office. Every time I'd tried to call Hussain, his son, who told me his name was Haris, had blocked me. He acts as a kind of gatekeeper to his father. So I wasn't surprised to see Haris behind the reception desk of the hotel. I told him I was looking for his father.

"He's out of town," Harris said.

"So he owns this place, right?" I asked.

"No, I own it."

"You're his son, right?"

"Yes."

"And you own the hotel, and not your dad?"

"Well, I work for him."

"You work for him, but you own the hotel?"

"Yes."

"So you own this hotel but you work for your dad—at this hotel?"

"Yes."

It was the type of nonsensical information that always seems to surround Hussain. That's why it's difficult to parse truth from invention in the FBI informant's life story, which becomes amusing when you think about it, because the Justice Department puts Hussain on the witness stand and asks jurors—who know so little about him—to believe what he says.

Of course, Hussain never called me after my visit to his hotel. But I knew he was still working for the FBI, in some Muslim community somewhere in the United States. I just didn't know where. Then, little more than a year later, he resurfaced.

6. "TO CATCH THE DEVIL, YOU HAVE TO GO TO HELL"

Using informants with criminal backgrounds has long been a controversial FBI practice. The most famous example involves Boston gangster Whitey Bulger, who served as an FBI informant for nearly twenty years in exchange for federal law enforcement's not referring for prosecution his organization's criminal activities, which included extortion, loan sharking, bookmaking, hijacking, and the trafficking of guns and drugs. After losing his FBI protection in the mid-1990s and being indicted on federal racketeering charges, Bulger spent the next fifteen years as a fugitive from justice—twelve of them on the FBI's Most Wanted Fugitive List—before federal agents found him in Santa Monica, California, in 2011. Bulger, who was eighty-one years old at the time, had $800,000 in cash and a weapons arsenal in his apartment.[1] He has become legendary in the Bureau—a kingpin-turned-informant who committed crimes far more serious than the ones he dropped the dime on.

Since 9/11, there have been many instances of federal informants committing crimes worse than the ones they were helping to investigate. In South Florida in 2003, Luis Martinez—a Mariel boatlift refugee and career criminal who became a federal informant assisting with investigations of home invasions in which firearms were taken—murdered retired

Genovese crime family member Charlie Moretto in a man-
sion on Millionaire's Row in Lighthouse Point, in Broward
County.[2] Nearly a decade later, in 2011, across the country
in Seattle, a federal informant sexually abused an eighteen-
year-old woman while holding her prisoner for several days
in a cheap motel room.[3] These are but two examples of the
hundreds, if not thousands, of crimes, from fraud to murder,
committed by FBI informants in the last ten years. Some
have been reported and resulted in criminal charges, while
others were simply made to go away by the FBI or other
law enforcement agencies. There's a saying in the Bureau that
sums up the criminal tendencies of informants: "The only
problem worse than having an informant is not having an
informant."

The use of criminals as informants is due in large part to
a pervasive belief within the Bureau that only criminals can
catch other criminals, an idea summed up neatly by another
FBI saying: "To catch the devil, you have to go to hell." If an
agent can find a thug over whom he or she can hold criminal
or immigration charges, it puts that agent in a position of
control over someone who can navigate the depths of criminal hell for an investigation. This practice has only grown
since 9/11, and in particular since George W. Bush's 2004
presidential directive to increase the number of informants
used by federal law enforcement, which put substantial pressure on agents to recruit and use informants. This has in turn
brought more and more criminals, many of them violent offenders, under the contract employment of the FBI.

During a conversation in early 2011, I asked Dale Watson,
who had been the FBI's assistant director for counterterrorism
on September 11, 2001, about the Bureau's use of criminals
as informants. A slightly overweight man with short brown

hair, green eyes, blushed cheeks, and a faint Southern accent, Watson told me that the Bureau wants informants who have committed unprosecuted crimes, so that those crimes can then be used as leverage to control them. "The best informants are the ones you jam up on something," he said matter-of-factly, adding that it isn't in the FBI's best interests to focus on questions of whether it's proper to use a particular informant in an investigation. "That's up to the court," Watson said. "We use whatever means we need to, under the law, to develop a prosecutable case, and the Justice Department puts it in front of a jury." Watson's logic is emblematic of an FBI culture that shuns introspection in favor of efficiency. If a policy or tactic is legal and obtains the results the government desires, FBI agents aren't in the practice of debating whether it's ethical, or even fair. And with overall federal conviction rates above 90 percent every year since 2001—in addition to a nearly perfect record in terrorism cases that go to trial—there's little motivation for the FBI to question its investigative tactics.[4]

But that could change. On Capitol Hill, an effort is underway to reform undercover investigations and introduce congressional accountability for the actions of federal informants. In 2011, U.S. Representative Stephen F. Lynch of Massachusetts sponsored the Confidential Informant Accountability Act, which would require federal law enforcement agencies to report to Congress twice a year on all serious crimes, authorized or unauthorized, committed by informants. Until that or similar legislation passes, no formal accountability system exists for the FBI and other federal law enforcement agencies in their use of criminals as informants. In addition, no meaningful oversight occurs in monitoring the targets of FBI investigations, questioning whether those individuals should even be the focus of informant-led stings in the first place, as well as the propriety of going after people who lack the capacity—financial or mental—to commit serious crimes. Because of this lack of oversight and accountability, the Bureau can use criminals in sting operations against easily susceptible targets without facing any kind of adverse consequences.

Take, for example, a sting case that began just months after the World Trade Center fell and involved two FBI informants, one with a long trail of debts, the other with an extensive rap sheet. The sting began when FBI informant Mohamed Alanssi entered House of Knowledge, an Islamic bookstore in New York City, in early 2002. Alanssi, a Yemeni, was a well-spoken man who had worked at the U.S. Embassy in Sana in the mid-1970s coordinating travel for State Department staff. However, his tenure at the U.S. Embassy had been rocky, and he was fired twice for reasons that have never been disclosed. "Let's just say that the embassy found him to be untrustworthy," said Mohammed Almelahi, an embassy accountant.[5] Alanssi moved briefly to Saudi Arabia, where he started a travel agency that failed, before returning to Yemen and defaulting on a $71,700 loan he'd taken out on his home. A year before 9/11, with his debts piling up in Yemen, Alanssi moved to New York City, where he opened a travel agency out of a small second-story office on Court Street in Brooklyn. Just as in Yemen, Alanssi racked up unpaid bills in Brooklyn.

But his fortunes changed two months after 9/11 when FBI agents began cracking down on *hawaladars*, brokers connected to an underground global banking network whose roots date back to the eighth-century Islamic world. In the *hawala* system, money can be transferred without having to be moved physically or electronically. Let's say a man in Brooklyn needs to send money to a relative in Islamabad,

Pakistan. He can give the money to a local hawaladar, who will take a small fee and then contact another hawaladar in Islamabad, instructing that hawaladar on the amount of money to be remitted and the password the recipient must provide for collection. The whole system, out of the reach of government regulators, is based on trust. The first hawaladar never sends money to the second; there is an implicit expectation that the money will be repaid later on, likely through a cash transaction in the opposite direction.

Immediately after 9/11, FBI agents suspected hawaladars in Brooklyn's Yemeni community of helping to finance international terrorism, and during their investigation, agents happened across Alanssi. In the aftermath of the devastating terrorist attacks, FBI agents were desperate to recruit informants who could infiltrate Muslim communities. In spite of his debts and problematic employment history with the State Department, Alanssi quickly became one of the FBI's early counterterrorism stars, and one of its best-paid informants. Alanssi was ultimately able to deliver several prize catches for the FBI, including Sheik Mohammed Ali Hassan al-Moayad, who the U.S. government believed was raising money for Al Qaeda in Brooklyn's Yemeni community. [6]

In the 2002 sting, Alanssi pretended to be a customer and asked bookstore owner Abdulrahman Farhane if he could help him purchase weapons and other equipment for Islamic fighters in the Middle East. Farhane demurred and instead introduced Alanssi to a man named Tarik Shah, who taught martial arts at a nearby studio. A Sunni Muslim whose parents were members of the Nation of Islam, Shah was an accomplished jazz musician who toured in Japan with Betty Carter and played at Bill Clinton's 1992 presidential inauguration. Alanssi would spend the next two years with Shah, and while the FBI obtained recordings of Farhane and Shah discussing how they could transfer money overseas, the government didn't have enough for an indictment. So the FBI turned to a second informant, Theodore Shelby, a former Black Panther who had scratched out a living stealing from drug dealers before going to prison for a series of tollbooth robberies.[7] Shelby, who went by the name Saeed Torres when working as an informant, agreed to cooperate with the FBI in exchange for early release from prison.

Shelby's relationship with Shah began when he asked for a bass lesson. This led to Shelby renting the bottom floor of a three-family house in the Bronx that Shah's mother owned (Shah lived on the second floor). Living right below his target, Shelby was able to secretly record conversations that portrayed Shah as a man obsessed with his martial arts prowess as well as a desire to train Muslims in hand-to-hand combat.[8] In one exchange, Shah pointed to the sharp pin his bass rested on. He could kill someone with that, he said. "Flip, pop, pop, right in the middle of your head," Shah explained.[9]

On December 16, 2003, Shah told Shelby that he was interested in training Muslims for jihad. His technique, he said, was "deadly and dangerous." Shelby in turn told Shah he had access to a warehouse in Long Island. Pleased, Shah said he'd need to hang some tires there. "I teach brothers how to use swords and machetes," he said, explaining his need for rubber. The informant then told Shah that he knew an Al Qaeda recruiter, and FBI agents turned to a seasoned hand for the final part of the sting.

On March 3, 2004, Shah and Shelby took a train to meet with the so-called recruiter. Shah didn't know that the operative—a squat, Arabic-speaking man with short-cropped black hair and a round face—was undercover FBI special agent Ali Soufan, a John O'Neill protégé. Shah told Soufan that he had a friend, a doctor named Rafiq Sabir, who lived in Palm Beach County, Florida, and had gone to the "mountains"—which FBI agents believed to mean terrorist training camps in Afghanistan. Soufan, in turn, told Shah that many of Al Qaeda's hand-to-hand combat trainers had been detained at Guantanamo Bay, and as a result, he and his friend were needed urgently. That's when Shah pulled out prayer beads and demonstrated how he could strangle a man to death using them. "Since I was pretty young, this has always been one of my dreams," Shah said of joining Al Qaeda.[10]

On April 1, 2004, Shah traveled with Soufan to meet with Sabir in Florida. At the meeting, Shah told Soufan that he wanted to learn about chemical weapons, explosives, and firearms, while Sabir talked about a recent trip he had taken to the Middle East, where he had worked at a Saudi military base in Riyadh. After their conversation, Soufan led both men in oaths to Al Qaeda—which would provide enough evidence to win convictions for the government. Days after the oath, the FBI arrested both men, Shah in New York and Sabir in Florida. Shah pleaded guilty and was sentenced to fifteen years in prison, while Sabir was convicted at trial and received twenty-five years.

Shah is currently in federal prison in Petersburg, Virginia. His elderly mother, Marlene Jenkins, lives in Albany—less than a mile, by coincidence, from the convenience store that FBI superinformant Shahed Hussain owned and the Department of Motor Vehicles office where he ran the scams that first brought him to the Bureau's attention. I visited Jenkins at her home in February 2011. She was seventy-five at the time, and she kept her small house tidy and spotless. All of the living room furniture was wrapped in firm plastic. Eager to talk about her son, she pulled out photos of Shah holding his bass or playing at jazz clubs. Her son wasn't dangerous, she maintained. His only crime was running his big mouth. "No weapons, no bomb," Jenkins said of the government's case against her son.[11] "It was just talk. They never did anything. People just talk all the time. But they don't follow through." Jenkins believes the two paid FBI informants entrapped her son.

Theodore Shelby has continued to work as an FBI informant in counterterrorism cases. But Mohamed Alanssi, who was paid more than $100,000 for his work as an informant, left the Bureau's employment in spectacular fashion. On November 16, 2004, Alanssi, then fifty-two years old, faxed a letter to the *Washington Post* and the New York office of the FBI, saying that he was about to "burn my body at an unexpected place."[12] He complained that the FBI was unwilling to provide security for his family in Yemen, who were in danger, he claimed, following his being named as a witness—and revealed as an informant—in the trial of Sheik Mohammed Ali Hassan al-Moayad. "Why you don't care about my life and my family's life?" Alanssi wrote in his letter, which was addressed to FBI Special Agent Robert Fuller, the same agent who was in charge of Shahed Hussain in Newburgh.

At 2:05 p.m., dressed in a pressed suit and tie, Alanssi walked up to the White House's northwest guardhouse on Pennsylvania Avenue and asked to have a note delivered to President George W. Bush. The guards turned him away. Alanssi, who was soaked in gasoline, then pulled out a lighter and ignited his clothing. Secret Service agents wrestled him to the ground and put out the flames with an extinguisher. Alanssi wound up with burns over 30 percent of his body.

Alanssi's self-immolation made the front page of the *Washington Post* and received extensive coverage on cable news and in the world media. As a result of the publicity, prosecutors didn't want to call him as a witness in the trial of al-Moayad, forcing defense lawyers to bring him to court instead, where he wore a flesh-colored glove on his right hand to cover up the burn wounds.[13]

The sour ending to the government's relationship with Alanssi had no effect on the FBI's continued use of terrorism informants with questionable backgrounds. Following Alanssi's dramatic exit from its informant ranks, the Bureau began to bring in informants with even more checkered pasts. While Alanssi had left a trail of debts and unanswered questions about what he'd done to be fired twice from his job at the U.S. Embassy in Yemen, this new crop of terrorism informants included fraud artists, drug dealers, thieves, and gunmen. Shahed Hussain, an accused murderer and con man, was among them.

At the beginning of 2006, the FBI became so desperate to infiltrate what agents believed was a terrorist cell in the suburbs of Philadelphia that they freed one Muslim from probation and released another from jail just to use as informants.

The story of that case began in New Jersey on January 31, 2006, when Mohamed Shnewer dropped off a homemade video to a Circuit City store in Mount Laurel in order to have it converted to a DVD. The FBI had never heard of Shnewer, but that afternoon, Brian Morgenstern, a clerk at Circuit City, called federal authorities and explained that a video he was converting contained "disturbing" images.[14] In the video, recorded on January 3, 2006, ten men in their twenties, wearing camouflage and fatigues, fired rifles in a wooded area in

Pennsylvania. As they fired, they shouted, "*Allahu Akbar!*" or "God is great!" In addition to Shnewer, the men in the video included Dritan, Shain, and Eljvir Duka—brothers and illegal immigrants—and Serdar Tatar. Shnewer was Eljvir's brother-in-law.

The video prompted the FBI to start an investigation through the Joint Terrorism Task Force, and the Bureau turned to two hardened criminals to infiltrate the group as informants. The primary informant, Mahmoud Omar, had entered the United States illegally and was on probation for bank fraud when the FBI approached him. The other informant, Besnik Bakalli, was in a Pennsylvania jail cell awaiting deportation to Albania, where he was wanted for a shooting.

In March 2006, Omar, who claimed to have served in the Egyptian military, befriended Shnewer, an overweight, socially awkward twenty-year-old with an interest in jihadi videos. At the same time, Bakalli began spending time with some of Shnewer's associates, including Eljvir Duka. Four months later, on July 28, 2006, the FBI got its first break in the case when Serdar Tatar, whose family owned a pizza shop near the Fort Dix army base in New Jersey, asked Omar if he could fix a problem with his car. The informant took the vehicle to law enforcement officials, who found a fifty-round box of nine-millimeter ammunition in the car. Following this, Omar began to wear a wire, and on August 1, 2006, Shnewer was recorded telling the informant that he, Tatar, and the three Duka brothers were part of a group planning to attack the Fort Dix army base. He explained that they wanted to gather as many as seven men to kill at least one hundred soldiers using rocket-propelled grenades. They'd been training for the attack, Shnewer told the informant, and had a good reason for choosing Fort Dix as their target. "Why did I choose Fort Dix? Because I know that Serdar knows it like the palm of his hand," Shnewer said—a reference to Tatar's familiarity with the base from delivering pizzas there.[15] Shnewer asked Omar, the informant, to lead the attack, since he said he had military experience in Egypt.

Four days later, on August 5, Shnewer and Omar discussed tactics. "Maybe it's easy to hit them at night," Shnewer wondered. On August 11, Shnewer and Omar drove to Fort Dix to scope out the base. Shnewer liked what he saw. "This is exactly what we are looking for," he said. "You hit four, five, six Humvees and light the whole place up and retreat completely without any losses." Shnewer also told the informant he had a Serbian sniper from Kosovo—a man named Agron Abdullahu—who would help with the attack. While Shnewer and Omar were planning the attack, Bakalli, the second informant, was getting closer to the other members of the group.

However, a few months later, on November 15, 2006, the entire sting almost unraveled when Tatar—the one who supposedly knew his way around Fort Dix—called the Philadelphia Police Department. He explained how he'd been approached by Omar, and was worried that he was being set up in a terrorist plot. But Tatar never followed up with the police, and in the end chose not to back out of the plot. Even as he feared Omar was an informant or law enforcement officer, Tatar told him, "I'm gonna do it. Whether or not you are FBI, I'm gonna do it. Know why? It doesn't matter to me whether I get locked up, arrested . . . . I'm doing it in the name of Allah." He then handed Omar a map of Fort Dix, which Omar promptly turned over to FBI agents.

On January 19, 2007, the Dukas told Besnik Bakalli that they had a nine-millimeter handgun, an assault rifle, and a semiautomatic assault weapon, all of which they claimed to have gotten from Agron Abdullahu, the reported Serbian sniper. The group then made another trip to the Pennsylvania woods in February 2007 to fire semiautomatic rifles and shotguns. Later that month, Dritan Duka invited Omar to play paintball with them and asked if he knew how they could buy AK-47 assault rifles. On March 28, Omar provided a list of weapons and prices from his purported arms source. Shnewer said the pricing was "very good." Dritan Duka suggested that the better armed they were, the lower their chances of being caught, saying: "All the AKs, the M16s, and all the handguns . . . . I just want to be safe, brother . . . . I got five kids, so I don't wanna go down. People catch me, like, they think I'm a terrorist."

But if the Fort Dix Five, as the media would later dub them, were terrorists, they were coerced ones—pushed along by criminals who had personal interests in their prosecution. In several conversations, members of the group made comments that suggested they never intended to become violent. For example, one of the Duka cousins told Omar: "We are good the way we are. We are not going to kill anyone." A few days after that comment, when Omar tried to goad the group on by bringing up the story of an Ohio man who had been training with terrorists, Dritan Duka responded by saying that in the hysteria following 9/11, Muslims could be arrested just for talking, even if they didn't mean what they said. He likened it to their situation—how they were just bullshitting about an attack on Fort Dix. Similarly, following the paintball outing in February 2007, Bakalli asked the Duka cousins what they thought jihad meant. It didn't mean violence, they told him; it was a personal struggle against one's self and a struggle to live a good life. Less than a month after that statement, the FBI arrested the five men, charging them with attempted murder and conspiracy to commit murder. All five pleaded not guilty and went to trial.

In his opening remarks at the trial, Assistant U.S. Attorney William Fitzpatrick told the jury: "Their inspiration was Al Qaeda and Osama bin Laden. Their intention was to attack the U.S." The prosecution then played undercover recordings and the jihadi videos the Fort Dix Five had watched, trying to portray the New Jersey men as dangerous terrorists. Evan Kohlmann, the young terrorism expert with questionable credentials, served as a witness for the prosecution, telling the jury that the videos the defendants had watched were "some of the classics put out by [Al Qaeda]."[16]

The defense, in turn, attacked the credibility of the two paid informants—both of whom had money and freedom riding on a successful prosecution—and tried to minimize the videos by describing their viewing as nothing more than immature chest-thumping by the men. But the key to the whole case—and the key to other successful terrorism sting prosecutions since then—was the fact that the prosecution didn't need to prove that the Fort Dix Five *would* have carried out their attack plans. The conspiracy—that the men so much as talked about it and planned for it—was all prosecutors needed to prove them guilty of conspiracy to murder U.S. officials. In his closing remarks, Fitzpatrick emphasized this to the jury: "We don't even have to prove that they intended to kill [soldiers] in the United States . ... As long as the conspiracy exists, and as long as within New Jersey at least one overt act occurs, it doesn't matter if the object of the conspiracy was to kill a soldier in Delaware, or in Pennsylvania, or in Iraq, or in Afghanistan. The conspiracy is the charge. The conspiracy is the heart and soul."[17]

The jury agreed, convicting the Fort Dix Five of conspiracy to commit murder, though it acquitted them of the charge of attempted murder. The three Duka cousins and Shnewer received life sentences, while Tatar received thirty-three years. Agron Abdullahu, the reported Serbian sniper who was only peripherally connected to the plot, pleaded guilty to conspiracy to provide firearms, for selling guns to the Dukas. He received twenty months in prison. For a successful prosecution, the two informants, Mahmoud Omar and Besnik Bakalli, freed from probation and jail respectively to serve the government, were paid performance incentives whose amounts have never been disclosed.

By training and firing weapons in the woods of Pennsylvania, the Fort Dix Five demonstrated capacity for violence—even if the evidence made public at their trial suggested they were just a bunch of young guys full of bluster—thus making the FBI's infiltration of the group by informants at least somewhat understandable. In many other terrorism stings, however, while the target hasn't demonstrated the slightest inclination toward criminal behavior, the informant who leads the plot has a long and violent criminal history.

A good example of this occurred in Rockford, Illinois. Working at a video game store, Derrick Shareef was twenty-two years old, broke, and didn't have a place to live when an FBI informant approached him in September 2006, offering the use of a car, a place to live, and free meals. It was the day before Ramadan, and Shareef, who'd been ostracized by his family since converting to Islam at the age of fifteen, saw the offer as an act of God. The informant, whose name has never been revealed, had been convicted of armed robbery in 1991 and possession of a stolen vehicle in 1997, as well as being a former member of the Four Corner Hustlers, a mostly black street gang known for its brutality on Chicago's West Side.[18]

While they lived together, the informant and Shareef discussed what they believed were injustices in the Muslim community. Their conversations turned to conspiracy and violence, with the two deciding to plot an attack in the United States—a demonstration, they told each other, that would shake the American people. On November 26, 2006, Shareef told the informant he wanted to attack "some type of City Hall type stuff right now, federal courthouses." The informant asked Shareef how he intended to pull off such an attack. "You go in there and you clock the first three niggers at the door—everything else is gonna have to be tactical," Shareef said, as if he had experience in combat tactics, adding: "I just want to smoke a judge."[19]

The informant told Shareef that he knew an arms dealer, and if Shareef was interested in purchasing weapons for an attack, he could arrange a meeting. The informant also recommended that they target a shopping mall. "We gotta look at it this way," he told Shareef. "We want to disrupt Christmas." This idea excited Shareef, and the informant said that they should purchase grenades for the attack. Shareef agreed. The informant then stressed that he was "down" for the attack. "I swear by Allah, man, I'm down for it too," Shareef told the informant. "I'm down to live for the cause and die for the cause, man."

Later, the informant told Shareef that he had ordered eleven "pineapples"—their code word for grenades—"at fifty bucks a pop." Since Shareef had no idea how to use a grenade, the informant had to give him a tutorial, explaining how to detonate one and how the timing mechanism worked. They then prepared for the shopping mall attack, creating video statements on December 2, 2006. While Shareef was so eager for the attack that he kept assuring the informant of his commitment, he also made it clear that he couldn't have hatched the plot without the informant's help. "I'm ready, man," he said. "I probably would have eventually ended up just stabbing the shit outta some Jews or something. Just stabbing them niggers with a steak knife."

Though the informant had brought Shareef along in the plot, the case was still weak. While the FBI had the makings of a conspiracy charge, since Shareef and the informant had discussed an attack, Shareef still hadn't participated in a overt act to further the conspiracy. He hadn't done any surveillance, and nothing he had done suggested he was ready to take the plot beyond talk. To get things moving, the FBI instructed the informant to suggest to Shareef that he purchase some grenades. However, Shareef didn't have any money. In fact, the only thing he had of value was a set of stereo speakers worth about one hundred dollars. The informant told Shareef that he could broker a trade with the arms dealer—the speakers in exchange for grenades and a nine-millimeter handgun. "I think what he gonna do is just take the speakers and say, 'Even,'" the informant said. While the claim was ridiculous—no arms dealer would accept used stereo speakers in exchange for black-market weapons—Shareef, evidencing his gullibility, never questioned it. The informant then put Shareef in touch with his arms dealer friend, who was an undercover FBI agent.

On December 4, 2006, the undercover agent and Shareef talked on the phone and agreed to meet at a store parking lot on Walton Road in Rockford, where the deal went just as the informant said it would. Shareef handed over the speakers, and the undercover FBI agent gave him a box containing four inert grenades and a nine-millimeter handgun. FBI agents immediately arrested Shareef, who pleaded guilty to one count of attempting to use a weapon of mass destruction. At the age of twenty-three, he was sentenced to thirty-five years in prison.

Since Shareef never went to trial, the identity of the informant and his motives for serving the government weren't revealed. But available court records suggest that the informant would have been a problematic one for the FBI had he needed to testify. In addition to the convictions for armed robbery and car theft, the informant owed $16,000 in child support—which was the exact amount the FBI paid him for his role in the terrorism sting—demonstrating his financial interest in seeing Shareef sent to prison. The conviction the criminal-turned-informant helped the FBI secure was Shareef's first; as a matter of fact, aside from a traffic violation for driving without insurance, it was the first time he had ever been charged with any kind of crime.[20]

In spite of their criminal pasts, no evidence indicates that the informants in the cases of either the Fort Dix Five or Derrick Shareef committed any crimes while working for the FBI. However, it is not unusual for informants with criminal backgrounds to revert to their illegal ways while employed by the Bureau. That's what happened in Decatur, Illinois, when an informant who had spent time in prison on drug charges met a man named Michael Finton.

Finton was a white man in his twenties who went by the name Talib Islam, which he adopted after converting to Islam while in prison for robbery. During his probation, Finton failed to notify his parole officer of an address change. The parole violation prompted a routine search of his home and car, and during the search, probation officers found Islamic writings and letters Finton had sent to John Walker Lindh, the American who went to prison for joining the Taliban after 9/11. Finton's bank records showed an incoming wire transfer from a man in Saudi Arabia named Asala Hussein Abiba. The officers also discovered evidence that Finton had gone to Saudi Arabia for a month in April 2008.

The suspicious probation officers turned this information over to the FBI, whose agents brought in an informant to get closer to Finton. "To my knowledge, the motive of the CHS to assist in this investigation is solely hope for monetary payment," FBI Special Agent Trevor S. Stalets wrote in an affidavit, using the acronym for "confidential human source," the FBI's term of art for informant.[21] The confidential human source and Finton became fast friends, with Finton telling the informant he wanted to receive military training so that he could fight against Israel. He also told the informant about his trip to Saudi Arabia, which had been paid for by a sheikh he met on the Internet whose daughter he was now engaged to marry. On December 29, 2008, Finton explained to the informant that he wanted to "secure his place in paradise by becoming a mujahid." The informant in turn told Finton he knew someone who could help, and Finton sent an introductory email to the informant's contact. Finton didn't know that the contact was an undercover FBI agent.

At the same time he was targeting Finton, the FBI informant was involved in criminal activity of his own—real crimes in this case, not imaginary plots. Sources told the FBI that the informant was dealing drugs while working for the government—information the Bureau could not confirm independently but which it viewed as credible enough to report it to the court in an affidavit. Yet the informant's alleged drug slinging while on the government payroll wasn't enough for the FBI to call off the terrorism sting against Finton.

On May 6, 2009, the undercover FBI agent met Finton in a hotel in Collinsville, Illinois, eighty miles south of Springfield. There, the agent told Finton he was an Al Qaeda operative recruiting terrorists in the United States. Finton expressed his desire "to receive military-type training." Over the next few weeks, Finton and the undercover agent discussed possible targets before settling on the Paul Findley Federal Building in Springfield, a gray, three-story limestone building that houses the U.S. courthouse and is named after a former congressman from Illinois.

Finton explored the building for reconnaissance. Deciding that a backpack bomb would not be suitable, he told his supposed terrorist friend that a car bomb would work best. The undercover FBI agent said Al Qaeda could provide a car bomb to be parked in front of the building. Finton then recorded a video. "Muslims would fight back to stop America at any cost," he said, explaining that he was not bombing the building for financial gain but in the hopes that "the big bully Israel would not be there anymore."[22] At the same time he was moving forward in the plot, Finton also began to wonder if he was being set up—but he quickly reasoned away that concern, telling the informant that he didn't think law enforcement authorities were that smart.

On September 23, 2009, the informant drove Finton from Decatur to Springfield, where Finton met with the undercover FBI agent and picked up a van with an inert bomb in the back. The undercover agent showed Finton how to detonate the supposed bomb once the vehicle was in position. Finton then drove the van to the Paul Findley Federal Building and parked it in front. He got out of the vehicle, walked to a safe distance, and dialed on his cell phone the number that he believed would detonate the bomb. Nothing happened, and FBI agents arrested him. Finton pleaded guilty to attempted murder and attempted use of a weapon of mass destruction. He was sentenced to twenty-eight years in prison. The drug-dealing informant was never identified in court records.

The Finton sting was not the only instance in which an informant had problems with drugs and the FBI chose to ignore them. In the case of Rezwan Ferdaus, a twenty-six-year-old living in a suburb outside Boston, the informant had a problem with heroin to which the Bureau turned a blind eye. As part of an FBI sting, Ferdaus, a bright young man who had graduated from Northeastern University with a degree in physics, met two people—one an informant, the other an FBI agent—who he believed were Al Qaeda operatives. The disgruntled Ferdaus told the agent and the informant he wanted to launch an attack against the United States. However, the idea he came up with—destroying the gold dome of the U.S. Capitol Building by using a remote-controlled model airplane loaded with grenades—seemed so out of touch with reality as to raise significant questions about his mental state.[23]

The informant in the case, a man known as Khalil, had difficulties of his own, including a heroin habit he hadn't told the FBI about. Khalil inadvertently revealed his drug problem to the Bureau when he showed up on a secret recording of another, unrelated case, buying heroin. Despite catching him on tape, the FBI didn't terminate Khalil from its informant ranks.

Khalil's heroin problem carried over to the Ferdaus case, where he was overheard on an undercover recording saying he was sick and needed drugs. (He was also caught shoplifting while wearing an FBI wire, despite being paid $50,000 and being given the use of an apartment for his work as an informant.) As a result of that recording, Khalil's drug habit came up as an issue in a November 2011 pretrial hearing for Ferdaus.

"What steps did you take to ensure he wasn't using heroin?" Ferdaus's public defender, Miriam Conrad, asked FBI Special Agent John Woudenberg.

"He was much scrutinized," Woudenberg said. "He was under the microscope."

"Did you give him a drug test?"

"No," Woudenberg admitted.[24]

Ferdaus pleaded guilty to attempting to damage and destroy a federal building by means of an explosive, and attempting to provide material support to terrorists and a terrorist organization.[25] He received seventeen years in prison.

The FBI's search for would-be terrorists is so all-consuming that agents are willing to partner with the most heinous of criminals if they appear able to deliver targets. That's what happened in Seattle, Washington, in the summer of 2011, when agents chose to put on the government payroll a convicted rapist and child molester.

The investigation began on June 3, 2011, when a man contacted the Seattle Police Department and told them that he had a friend named Abu Khalid Abdul-Latif who was interested in attacking Joint Base Lewis-McChord in Tacoma, Washington. The tipster told police that Abdul-Latif had already recruited an associate, a man named Walli Mujahidh. Seattle police referred the caller to the FBI, whose agents quickly enlisted him as an informant and launched a full investigation of Abdul-Latif and Mujahidh.

Based on these initial actions, it was clear that the FBI believed it was dealing with two dangerous potential terrorists. But in reality, what it had were two financially troubled men with histories of mental problems. Abdul-Latif, whose birth name was Joseph Anthony Davis, had spent his teenage years huffing gasoline and once told a psychologist he heard voices and saw things that weren't there. When he was twenty-three, he tried to commit suicide by overdosing on pills intended to treat seizure disorders, later telling a psychologist that he "felt lonely and had no use to live."[26] His partner in the supposed terrorist plot, thirty-one-year-old Mujahidh, whose name was Frederick Domingue Jr. before his conversion to Islam, had been diagnosed with schizoaffective disorder, which causes mood swings and abnormal thoughts.[27] Dorothy Howard, who met Mujahidh through her daughter when they lived in Pomona, California, remembered him as sweet-natured but gullible, someone who was trying hard to get a handle on his mental problems but wasn't always successful. "Sometimes he would call me and say, 'Mrs. Howard, I really need my medications. Can you take me to the clinic?'" Howard recalled. "Sometimes they would keep him three or four days."[28]

The FBI's informant, whose name was not revealed, was the only source claiming that Abdul-Latif and Mujahidh were terrorists on the make. And the informant came with an outrageous story of his own. In addition to being a convicted rapist and child molester, according to government records, he had stolen thousands of dollars from Abdul-Latif in the past and had tried, but failed, to steal Abdul-Latif's wife as well.[29] The state of Washington had also classified the informant as a high-risk sex offender, and while working for the FBI, he was caught sending sexual text messages in violation of his parole—something he attempted to hide from agents by trying to delete the messages.[30] Despite what were obvious problems with the investigation from the start, the FBI gave the informant recording equipment and instructed him to move forward with the sting.

As Abdul-Latif and the informant discussed possible targets—after growing concerned that attacking a military base would be too difficult, given the armed guards and fortification—it became clear that the Seattle man had no capacity to carry out a terrorist attack. In fact, Abdul-Latif had little capacity for anything, since he had only $800 to his name, and his only asset was a 1995 Honda Passport with 162,000 miles.[31] In addition, his supposed accomplice, Mujahidh, was still in Southern California. But his friend, the informant, said he could provide everything they would need for the attack, including M13 assault rifles, rocket-propelled grenades, and bulletproof vests.[32] That Abdul-Latif didn't have much money and didn't know anyone who could provide him with weapons strongly suggested that the plot was nothing more than talk, and would have stayed that way had the FBI not gotten involved.

After scuttling the idea to attack Joint Base Lewis-McChord, Abdul-Latif and the informant settled on a plan to attack a Seattle processing station for incoming troops, where most of the people would be unarmed. "Imagine how many young Muslims, if we're successful, will try to hit these kinds of centers. Imagine how fearful America will be, and they'll know they can't push Muslims around," Abdul-Latif said. On June 14, 2011, Abdul-Latif and the informant purchased a bus ticket for Mujahidh to travel to Seattle from Los Angeles. Needing to select a password that would allow Mujahidh to pick up the ticket at the station, Abdul-Latif initially suggested "jihad." He and the informant laughed about the password choice before Abdul-Latif decided on "OBL," for Osama bin Laden.

A week later, Mujahidh arrived in Seattle, and the three men drove to a parking garage to inspect the weapons the informant had procured. Inside a duffel bag were three assault rifles. Mujahidh took hold of one of the guns, aimed, and pulled the trigger. Abdul-Latif inspected one of the other rifles. "This is an automatic?" he asked. The informant then showed him how to switch on the rifle's setting for automatic firing. At that point, FBI agents rushed into the garage and arrested Abdul-Latif and Mujahidh. The two men were charged with conspiracy to murder officers and agents of the United States, conspiracy to use a weapon of mass destruction, and four firearms counts. The FBI paid the informant $90,000 for his work on the case.[33]

Michele Shaw was the public defender appointed to Mujahidh. When she first met him inside a jail in Seattle, she couldn't believe he was the man the government had portrayed as a dangerous terrorist. "He is the most compliant client I have ever worked with in my twenty-two years of practicing law and so appreciative of our weekly visits," Shaw said. From the start, Shaw knew she had a mental health case on her hands, not a terrorist case. Mujahidh was easily susceptible to the informant, she believed, because he had a history of relying on others to help him separate fantasy from reality. But the judge in the case didn't agree. "Walli's mental health issues in my opinion are huge and looming large, but the court stated this week on the record that my client's mental health issues are a very tiny part of this case," Shaw told me in October 2011. Unable to use mental health in an entrapment defense, Shaw reluctantly recommended that Mujahidh plead guilty. He agreed, and was sentenced to twenty-seven to thirty-two years in prison. For his part, Abdul-Latif pleaded not guilty and is awaiting trial. Had it not been for a rapist and child molester fishing for a payday, Abdul-Latif and Mujahidh would likely be today where they were in June 2011—two Americans you'd never hear about, trapped on the margins of a society to which they posed no threat.

Abu Khalid Abdul-Latif and Walli Mujahidh became terrorists because the FBI and one of its informants had incentives for making the pair into terrorists. The informant's incentive was monetary, while the FBI agents who supervised the sting were under intense pressure from their higher-ups to build a terrorism case. At no point during the sting operation did anyone question whether someone like Abdul-Latif was more despondent loser than scary mass murderer. That is a problem inherent in today's terrorism sting operations: the FBI and its informants are under pressure—albeit for different reasons—to see terrorists, even where none exist.

Since informants have vested interests in seeing their targets convicted—with criminal informants often having their own personal freedom on the line—it's the FBI's responsibility to ensure that these interests do not influence investigations. If the Bureau is following "the book" during an investigation, agents will give an informant tasking orders before each meeting between the informant and the targets. These orders will include what the informant should discuss and how he should behave during the meeting. Ideally, the meeting with the targets should be taped, giving the FBI an indisputable record of what was said. At regular intervals, FBI agents should also subject their informant to a polygraph test to make sure he isn't lying or withholding information. If the informant fails the polygraph, or engages in criminal behavior not authorized by the FBI, agents are supposed to cut him from the ranks.

However, the FBI doesn't always work by the book. We know this because the Bureau has documented many occasions when it doesn't play by its own rules. Elie Assaad, the informant in the Florida stings involving Imran Mandhai and the Liberty City Seven, lied during a polygraph examination in Chicago yet continued to work as an FBI informant. In the Michael Finton case, the FBI had credible information that its informant was dealing drugs yet continued to use him until the final day of the sting operation. The informant in the Rezwan Ferdaus case was caught on an FBI video purchasing heroin and still the Bureau continued to pay him for his work. These informants were allowed to lead terrorism stings because the pressure to find would-be terrorists is so great that it's created a precarious situation in which FBI agents identify loudmouths on the fringes of society and through, elaborate sting operations involving informants, many with criminal backgrounds, transform these powerless braggarts into dangerous terrorists engaged in horrifying plots to bomb buildings, public squares, and subway stations.

7. NOT CAUGHT ON TAPE

Because so many of the informants that the FBI uses in terrorism stings are men with histories of crime, fraud, and deception—in short, not the most credible people to put on a witness stand during a trial—the Bureau relies heavily on secretly recording the conversations between its informants and the individuals they target. When an informant lacks credibility or has a financial interest in gaining a conviction, a taped conversation showing the target going along with the plot can often make up for those deficiencies with a jury. As a result, in the terrorism sting cases that have gone to trial since 9/11, prosecutors have played hours of taped conversations between informants and targets for juries.

However, in analyzing these cases, I noticed a disturbing pattern of conversations between informants and targets not being recorded at the most suspicious of times. These "missing recordings" seem to occur at either the beginning of a sting, when informants are establishing their relationships with targets—a period of time defense lawyers consider crucial to determining whether the government induced or entrapped the defendant—or when the target is thinking of backing out of the plot or otherwise doing something that has the potential to undermine the government's case. No matter what part of a sting goes unrecorded, the government routinely blames "recorder malfunction" for the lapse.

The most egregious example of the mysterious and persistent FBI trend of recorder malfunction happened when two separate terrorism sting cases, located 2,800 miles apart from each other, converged in a most unexpected way in 2010. The first sting centered on an Oregon party boy who developed a peculiar hatred for the United States. Mohamed Osman Mohamud, a young Somali American, attended Oregon State University and lived in Corvallis, a college town about eighty-five miles south of Portland. He prayed at the Salman al-Farisi mosque, but many of his fellow congregants kept their distance from him, as Mohamud pushed an extreme, hundred-year-old Sunni brand of Islam known as Salafism—whose adherents, among them Osama bin Laden and other Al Qaeda leaders, seek to emulate the ways of the Prophet Mohammed and the earliest days of Islam. Mohamud, however, led a life at odds withof his religion, drinking alcohol and engaging in premarital sex, two activities prohibited under most interpretations of the Koran.

It was Mohamud's partying that first brought him to the attention of the FBI. On the day after Halloween 2009, a woman reported to the Oregon State Police that Mohamud had raped her after a party the night before. Other students at the party told police that Mohamud and the woman had been together, dancing, flirting, and drinking, and at the end of the night, they had left together. Nothing seemed to be wrong between them, the witnesses said. But the next morning, the woman told the police that she believed she had been drugged—a stranger, she said, had given her a beer at the party that might have been spiked with something—

because she couldn't remember the details of having sex with Mohamud. (A test for any type of date rape drugs later came back negative.)

That evening, Oregon State Police asked Mohamud, then eighteen years old, to come to the campus police station for questioning. At the station, Mohamud told police he hadn't drugged or raped the woman, but said that they had gone to the party and then had consensual sex afterward. Police released Mohamud without charging him, but the next day, they called him back to the station to submit to a polygraph examination, which Mohamud agreed to. What he didn't know as he took the test was that FBI agents were watching from another room, where they heard Mohamud discuss his personal background, educational plans, family, and opinions of Somalia. The agents discovered that Mohamud was nervous about the prospect that his family would find out about his partying as a result of the rape investigation. "Mohamud is very concerned that his parents will freak out if they find out about the investigation or his use of drugs and alcohol," an FBI agent wrote in a report following the polygraph.[1]

During their questioning, police also asked Mohamud if an inspection of his laptop would reveal that he had researched date rape drugs. Mohamud said it wouldn't, and offered to allow the officers to search the laptop and his mobile phone. He wrote the following on a piece of paper: "I, Mohamed Osman Mohamud, give the Oregon State Police permission to seize and search my HP laptop computer and my Vodafone cell phone. No promises or threats have been made, and I give this consent freely." At the bottom of the page, below his signature and the signature of a witness, Mohamud wrote his laptop password: NorGrun. A state police computer analyst then copied the contents of the hard drive. What Mohamud didn't know was that the Oregon State Police later gave a disk to the FBI containing four folders from his hard drive as well as three pages of information from his cell phone. The Oregon State Police did not charge Mohamud with a crime following the rape investigation.[2]

To this day, the FBI has not disclosed why it was interested in a date rape suspect at Oregon State University and what information was on Mohamud's laptop and cell phone. The only fact the Bureau has revealed was that agents believed Mohamud was corresponding by email with a man in Northwest Pakistan, an area known for harboring terrorists, about a religious school in Yemen. In June 2010, more than six months after the rape investigation was closed, the FBI placed Mohamud on the federal no-fly list, at which time FBI agents interviewed him and he disclosed his intention to travel to Yemen. Later that month, on June 23, 2010, the FBI sting operation began in earnest.

The FBI believed that Mohamud had tried, but failed, to contact terrorists in Pakistan by email. An FBI informant then emailed Mohamud, pretending to be part of the terrorist group he'd reportedly been trying to reach, claiming to have received Mohamud's email address from the man he was trying to contact in Pakistan. The email read, in part and in all lowercase letters: "sorry for the delay in our communication, we've been on the move… are you still able to help the brothers?" In the "From" field was the name Bill Smith. Mohamud replied to the email, but was skeptical. Mohamud wanted "to make sure you are not a spy yourself," he wrote, and asked how Smith knew the man he'd been emailing. The undercover agent said he'd heard about Mohamud and received his email address from a mutual acquaintance, explaining cryptically that "a brother from Oregon who is now far away vouched for you." Mohamud agreed to meet with the man he believed was a terrorist in Portland on July 30, 2010.

At the meeting, Mohamud told an undercover agent that he had written some articles that had been published in *Jihad Recollections*, a seventy-page pro-Al Qaeda magazine that was run by Samir Khan, a then-twenty-two-year-old Pakistani American who lived in Charlotte, North Carolina.[3] (Khan later went to Yemen, where he became editor and publisher of Al Qaeda's *Inspire* magazine before being killed in a CIA drone strike on September 30, 2011, along with Al Qaeda propagandist Anwar al-Awlaki.)[4] The undercover FBI agent asked Mohamud what he was willing to do for the cause. Mohamud, who told the agent he "wanted to wage war in the U.S.," said he had been dreaming since he was fifteen years old about training with Al Qaeda in Yemen. If he wanted to get involved, the undercover agent told Mohamud, he had several options. He could pray five times a day and spread the word about Islam. He could continue studying, obtain his medical degree, and assist Al Qaeda as a doctor. He could raise money for terrorists overseas. Or he could become operational today, becoming a *shaheed*, or martyr. Mohamud chose the last option, saying that he wanted to put together an explosive device. The FBI agent told Mohamud to research possible targets, and that they'd meet again soon.

You would think that this critical encounter, the first in-person meeting between Mohamud and an undercover agent, would have been recorded, but it wasn't. The FBI did set up audio and video equipment, but due to a "malfunction," they weren't able to record the meeting. Therefore, all the information about what was said is based on the FBI agent's memory. Three weeks after that first meeting, Mohamud and the undercover agent met in a hotel room, and this time the recording equipment worked. Joining the FBI agent on this occasion was a second undercover agent who was posing as a weapons expert. Mohamud had done what he'd been told to do during the first meeting and came with a target in mind. "Pioneer Square, like, Portland, is, like, the main meeting—they have a twenty-sixth of November Christmas lighting and some 250,000 people come," Mohamud told the agents.[5]

The undercover agents asked Mohamud whether he was concerned that such a target could result in children being harmed or killed.

"That's what I'm looking for—a huge mass," he replied. "Attacked in their own element."

He'd push the button to detonate the bomb, the agents asked, even with children in the blast zone?

"Yes, I will push the button," he answered. "When I see the enemy of Allah, then you know their bodies are torn everywhere."

The undercover agents then told Mohamud they needed to discuss his idea with their superiors, a group they referred to as "the council."

The following month, September 2010, Mohamud met again with the two agents, who told him that the plan was moving forward and asked him to find a suitable area to plant the bomb near Pioneer Square and to purchase some components for the weapon, including two Nokia prepaid cell phones, a toggle switch, and a nine-volt battery connector. They explained to Mohamud how the bomb would work: he'd place it at the target, then dial a cell phone to detonate the weapon remotely. "When you dial that phone number, all of this is going to be gone," the second undercover agent said, referring to the two blocks around Pioneer Square.

However, despite his supposed desire to "wage war in the

U.S.," without the FBI's assistance, not only was Mohamud incapable of becoming a terrorist, since he lacked the skills necessary to build a bomb or the money and contacts to obtain weapons, he was on the verge of being thrown into the streets, as he was broke and running behind on the rent for his apartment. But the FBI didn't let those details stall the sting operation, as the undercover agents gave Mohamud $2,700 to cover his rent and another $110 for the bomb components.

On October 3, 2010, Mohamud dropped off the bomb components the undercover agents had requested. He also included a pack of gum with a handwritten note that read: "good luck with ur stereo system Sweetie. Enjoy the gum." The undercover agents picked up Mohamud that same day and drove him to a hotel. He described Pioneer Square to them in detail and then laid out a plan, including where they should plant the bomb. "It's gonna be a fireworks show," Mohamud said, showing agents pictures on his laptop of specific parking spots near Pioneer Square. He handed one of the agents a thumb drive with the images. The undercover agents then demonstrated to Mohamud how to detonate the bomb once he had it in position. "Do you remember when 9/11 happened, when those people were jumping from skyscrapers? I thought that was awesome," Mohamud told them. "I want to see that; that's what I want for these people. I want whoever is attending that event to leave, to leave either dead or injured." The undercover agents then recorded a video of Mohamud in which he threatened the United States, praised Allah, and read a poem.

On November 23, 2010, the undercover agents drove Mohamud to a storage unit they had rented to store the bomb materials, which included two barrels, a gasoline can, electrical wires, and a large box of screws. The three of them loaded the materials into the car, as well as reflective traffic markers, hard hats, safety glasses, vests, and gloves—all props for their cover.

Three days later, on November 26, the day of the Christmas tree lighting ceremony, the agents met Mohamud in a hotel room. The bomb was now assembled, though Mohamud didn't know it was inert. "Beautiful," he said of the weapon.

Mohamud and the undercover agents put the bomb in the car and drove to Pioneer Square, which was packed with people. They parked in one of the spots Mohamud had scouted out, then walked away from the vehicle, hard hats on so as not to raise suspicion. From a safe distance, Mohamud dialed the number that he believed would detonate the bomb. It failed. He dialed again. That's when FBI agents rushed in and arrested him. He kicked and screamed as he was surrounded. "*Allahu Akbar!*" he yelled. "God is great! *Allahu Akbar!*"

Announcements of terrorism stings always make for big news in the cities in which they occur, but Mohamud's arrest—involving a bomb plot in a crowded downtown area— drew more interest than most. It immediately made national news, splashing across the front pages of newspapers and getting covered by every broadcast and cable television news outlet in the country. The CBS *Evening News*, on November 27, 2010, showed footage of the Pioneer Square Christmas tree lighting ceremony. "Three, two, one," the crowd chanted, and then the massive tree lit up with lights. "The plan was to kill as many people as possible," CBS reporter Terry McCarthy said in the segment. "As thousands gathered for a tree lighting in Portland's Pioneer Square, nineteen-year-old Mohamed Osman Mohamud allegedly parked a van at the corner and attempted to detonate what he thought was a bomb."[6]

It is at this point that the Mohamud case converged with another FBI terrorism sting. Remember Antonio Martinez, the twenty-two-year-old who, with the help of an informant and an undercover FBI agent, tried to bomb a military recruiting center outside Baltimore? Nearly 3,000 miles away, Martinez was one of the millions of people who heard the news of Mohamud's arrest in Oregon. At the time, he was the unknowing target of an FBI sting that seemed just like the one that had ensnared Mohamud. After seeing news of Mohamud's arrest, Martinez became worried. Was he, too, being lured into a trap?

On November 27, 2010, the day after Mohamud's arrest, Martinez called his supposed terrorist contact, explaining that he had seen a story on the news about a man in Portland who had tried to detonate a bomb. The whole thing was a setup, Martinez told his contact, and he needed to know what was going on with their operation in Baltimore. "I'm not falling for no BS," he said.[7] The informant told Martinez that they should meet in person. He agreed. In the entire sting, this meeting was the most important one, as Martinez had grown suspicious and was ready to back out of the plot. What would the FBI operative say to Martinez to keep him on board? We'll never know because their conversation wasn't recorded. In an affidavit, the FBI blamed this on a recorder malfunction. Whatever the informant said during this unrecorded meeting, his words were enough to calm down Martinez. The next day, Martinez told the informant by phone: "I'm just ready to move forward." A week later, Martinez was arrested in a scene almost identical to Mohamud's. He tried to detonate a car bomb remotely. It failed. When he tried a second time, FBI agents arrested him.

If you take a close look at all the terrorism stings the FBI has engaged in since 9/11, you'll find missing recordings in nearly every one. While some are like the Martinez case— an important meeting going unrecorded due to what is reported to be recorder malfunction—more often, it is the initial encounters between the informant and the target, a critical time in a sting operation, that aren't recorded. In the Oregon case, Mohamud's first meeting with an undercover agent was not recorded—a problem the FBI attributed to the malfunctioning of its recording equipment. However, the same thing happened in the case of the Newburgh Four, in which Shahed Hussain spent four months with James Cromitie before the FBI decided to start recording their conversations. And even after recordings began in the Newburgh sting, the FBI elected not to tape some meetings, including vital ones such as when Hussain took the four men to dinner at a T.G.I. Friday's the night before the planned bombing and offered them money to carry forward with the plot.

Without recordings of these meetings, federal prosecutors must ask jurors to believe without question the recounting of events from an FBI informant—a man who usually has a past that includes some combination of violent crime, fraud, and deceit, and who has credibility only because he's been given the FBI's imprimatur. Defense lawyers then must convince the jury that the informant, despite his FBI association, is an untrustworthy, unsavory, and unfit witness. Halfway through the Newburgh trial, for example, defense lawyer Vincent L. Briccetti attempted in cross-examination to emphasize to the jury that without recordings, the government's informant, Shahed Hussain, couldn't be trusted to tell the truth.

"Now is it fair to say, sir, that a lot of what you testified to on direct in response to [the prosecutor's] questions related to tape recordings that were played for the jury?" Briccetti asked.

"Yes, sir," Hussain answered.

"But not everything that you testified to related to tape recordings, correct?"

"There was some that was testified that was not taped."

"Well, there were several months' worth of meetings between June and October of 2008 with my client, Mr. Cromitie, which were not taped, correct?"

"Yes, sir."

"And so you wanted the jury to trust you when you tell them what happened on those occasions, correct?"

"Yes, sir."

"And you're hoping they're going to believe what you have to say about all that, correct?"

"Yes, sir."[8]

In researching terrorism stings, the more I noticed missing recordings, the more I questioned current and former FBI agents about why some conversations are not recorded. Sometimes the recording equipment just doesn't work, they told me, or it's too dangerous to risk having the sting target discover that an informant or undercover agent is wearing a wire. "Every time you're doing an undercover, you have to factor in the level of danger to the informant or to the agent," J. Stephen Tidwell, the FBI's former executive assistant director, told me. "If you think there's a high risk, you're not going to use recording equipment."

Frances Townsend, President George W. Bush's national security advisor for terrorism, agrees with Tidwell's assessment. I met with Townsend, now a terrorism analyst for CNN, at her posh Manhattan office in early 2011, and asked her about the terrorism sting cases I'd reviewed in which meetings with targets were not recorded either intentionally or due to what appeared to be a suspiciously high rate of recorder malfunction. She couldn't address the specific cases I asked her about, since she hadn't reviewed them herself, but given her experience as federal prosecutor for organized crime in New York, she said she wasn't surprised by the missing recordings. "I can't tell you how many times I had FBI agents in front of me and I yelled, 'You have hundreds of hours of recordings, but you didn't record this meeting,'" she said. "But the reason isn't always nefarious. Sometimes, I admit, they might not record something intentionally. But more often than not, it's a technical issue. The equipment malfunctioned or the recording was inaudible."

I've never been satisfied with these kinds of explanations for missing recordings. As a journalist, I've recorded hundreds of interviews and meetings, using basic store-bought recording equipment. I've only experienced one recorder malfunction, and it was due to human error—I accidentally stopped the recorder. However, the FBI, with its sophisticated equipment, seems to experience these types of malfunctions regularly in terrorism stings.

In addition, the FBI's fear that informants or agents will be put in danger if the target discovers they're wearing recording equipment seems disingenuous since terrorism sting targets are dangerous only because the FBI says they are. Unlike in organized crime investigations, the FBI doesn't need to fear that terrorism sting targets, upon discovering that they are being set up, will pull out guns and start putting holes in informants and undercover agents. Terrorism sting targets rarely have weapons of their own, and most are scrawny young guys incapable of physically overpowering the average FBI agent.

One reason why missing recordings are so suspicious can be found in clues in the meetings between informants and targets that are recorded during FBI terrorism stings. It's not uncommon for informants to be caught on tape goading sting targets into moving forward with terrorist plots. "Do you want to call it off? You know, I'm not going to hold it against you," said the Seattle informant in the case involving the mentally ill men Abu Khalid Abdul-Latif and Walli Mujahidh, not so subtly trying to shame his targets.[9] If informants are willing to resort to taunts and bullying while wearing a wire, what do they say when the conversations aren't being recorded?

That's a question that James J. Wedick, the retired agent, often asks himself. During his thirty-four-year career with the FBI, Wedick went undercover in sting operations and later supervised agents working deep cover in sensitive criminal and drug cases. A thin, silver-haired man with a neatly groomed beard and round glasses, Wedick became interested in terrorism sting operations after he retired as a federal lawman and was hired as a consultant for the defense in a case in Lodi, California, in which an informant was caught on tape browbeating the target. In that case, a man in Oregon named Naseem Khan, who was working at a McDonald's and a convenience store, claimed that Al Qaeda second-in-command Ayman al-Zawahiri had been seen in Lodi, an agricultural town whose conservative Pakistani American community dates back to the early twentieth century—a claim the FBI later determined to be false. But based on that tip, the FBI recruited Khan to be an informant and paid him $300,000 over time to infiltrate mosques in Lodi.[10]

As he ingratiated himself into the city's Muslim community, Khan settled on two targets—ice cream truck driver

Umer Hayat and his son Hamid. FBI recordings suggested that Khan, whose informant code name was Wildcat, tricked Hamid into making incriminating statements and badgered him to attend a terrorist training camp. In 2003, Hamid traveled to Pakistan to meet his bride—it is not uncommon for Pakistani American families in Lodi to arrange marriages with families in Pakistan—but the girl in Pakistan rejected him. While his father and mother hustled around Rawalpindi, near Islamabad, to find a new bride for him, Hamid spent two months hanging out and doing nothing. Khan, frustrated that Hamid wasn't doing anything that could be used to build a prosecutable case, called him in Pakistan to intimidate him.

"When I God willing, when I come to Pakistan and I see you, I'm going to fucking force you—get you from your throat and fucking throw you in the madrassa," Khan said.

"I'm not going to go with that," Hamid replied.

"Oh, yeah, you will go. Yeah, you will go. You know what? Maybe I can't fight with you in America, but I can beat your ass in Pakistan so nobody's going to come to your rescue."[11]

Upon Hamid's return to the United States, FBI agents interrogated him. After initially denying during a five-hour grilling that he had attended a terrorist training camp, Hamid, worn down, eventually confessed, saying that he had attended a remote, forested camp in Pakistan. His father, Umer, later confessed to attending the same terrorist camp—but described a fantastical place where trainees wore masks "like ninja turtles" and attacked with swords dummies made to look like President George W. Bush, Secretary of Defense Donald Rumsfeld, and Secretary of State Colin Powell.[12] Umer later recanted his confession—saying he made it up after FBI agents refused to believe he didn't attend the camp, basing his fanciful descriptions on scenes from the movie *Teenage Mutant Ninja Turtles*, which he and his family had watched several times—and pleaded guilty to making a false statement to the FBI. Hamid Hayat went to trial and was found guilty of providing material support to terrorists and making false statements to the FBI. The government's case centered on Hamid's confession, which, in Wedick's view, came as a result of an illegal interrogation that involved intimidation and leading questions from an FBI agent. At the age of twenty-five, Hamid Hayat was sentenced to twenty-four years in prison.

After the Lodi case, Wedick was hired as a defense consultant for the Liberty City Seven in Miami. He's developed a keen interest in terrorism stings as a result, and is among the leading critics of the FBI's tactics and use of informants in these cases. He believes most of the targets of these stings lack the capacity to commit serious crimes on their own, let alone disastrous acts of terrorism. Mohamed Osman Mohamud in Portland was a perfect example. "This is a kid who, it can be reasonably inferred, barely had the capacity to put his shoes on in the morning," Wedick said.

Wedick doesn't believe that certain meetings aren't recorded in terrorism stings because the undercover activities are dangerous or the FBI's recording equipment has a high failure rate. There's another, more troubling explanation, he said. "With the technology the FBI now has access to—these small devices that no one would ever suspect are recorders or transmitters—there's no excuse not to tape interactions between the informant and the target," he said. "So why in many of these terrorism stings are meetings not recorded? Because it's convenient for the FBI not to record. They are paying informants huge sums of money and not monitoring them cor-

rectly. With some or many conversations not being recorded, I think it's apparent that the Bureau understands and is
aware of the problem, but is decidedly more interested in not
being caught flatfooted again about would-be and/or suspected terrorists and/or pathetic individuals doing whatever,
so we see rather aggressive informants suggesting or propos-
ing things J. Edgar Hoover never would have permitted, even
though he had informants reportedly under every nook and
cranny."

For the FBI, missing recordings—whether intentional
or the result of a recorder malfunction—come without
consequences. The Bureau can justify to the public
that intentionally not recording a meeting was due to
circumstances that made audio equipment too dangerous—
something that can be debated but not wholly proved or
disproved. Without a whistleblower, it's impossible to prove
that the FBI uses recorder malfunction as an excuse when it's
convenient for agents not to record a particular meeting, such
as when the target might be backing out of the plot or when
an informant's words, if recorded, could be construed at trial
as inducement.

The only possible consequence for the FBI comes in
court, when defense lawyers put informants on the witness
stand, bare to the jury in excruciating detail the informants'
past misdeeds, and then ask the jury to question whether certain meetings weren't recorded so they wouldn't hear the lies
the informants told to keep their targets engaged in a terrorist plot made possible by federal law enforcement in the
first place. Defense lawyers have repeatedly used unrecorded
conversations in trying to sell juries on entrapment defenses,
arguing that these meetings, if taped, would have contained
statements that proved the FBI's informant came up with

the idea for the plot and induced the targets into moving forward with it. But juries so far haven't bought that argument. Since 9/11, approximately fifty terrorism defendants have been involved in plots in which the informant could fairly be described as an agent provocateur, someone who provided not only the plan but also the means and opportunity for the terrorist plot. Ten of these defendants have formally argued entrapment during their trials.[13] Yet none of these defendants—and only a minority risk trial in the first place with the government's nearly perfect conviction rate and mandatory minimum sentences of twenty-five years in prison—were successful in convincing a jury that they'd been entrapped, that is, that they wouldn't have committed their crimes were it not for the FBI informant instigating them in the first place.

In talking about FBI terrorism stings among journalists, academics and the public, I am frequently asked why entrapment has never been an effective defense in the terrorism cases. I've struggled with the answer to this question. It's true that entrapment is a very risky legal strategy; after all, it requires the defendants to admit that they committed the crimes they are charged with and then hope that the jury will be sympathetic to their claim that the government induced them. It also requires the defense to disprove predisposition— the contention that the actions of the defendants prior to the introduction of the government informant suggested they would commit such a crime—and here the government has had little trouble in terrorism cases because so much today can be used to suggest predisposition. Watching jihadi videos, for example, as the Fort Dix Five did in New Jersey, or ranting about a hatred of Jews, as James Cromitie did in Newburgh, have both been viewed as evidence of predisposition. Of course, this is something of a simplification of a complicated legal subject. But with the entrapment defense, there's something unique to terrorism sting cases. Why, after all, has there never been an effective entrapment defense in a terrorism sting case?

David D. Cole has considered that question. A Georgetown University law professor who specializes in constitutional law and national security, Cole has paid close attention to the terrorism sting cases that have gone before juries. In early 2011, I asked him why terrorism defendants are unable to succeed with entrapment defenses when the evidence is clear that the informant provided the means and opportunity for the crime. "I think prosecutors overwhelm juries with evidence in these cases," Cole told me. "Jurors hear about a horrific plot to bomb the subway or a building, and they think, 'I ride the subway,' or, 'My brother works in that building.' Because the plot is so horrific, and people have memories of 9/11, the prosecution is able to overwhelm juries in such a way that prevents them from being sympathetic to an entrapment defense."

The FBI's success in terrorism trials has further emboldened the Bureau's use of sting operations. As with any organization, the FBI duplicates programs that are effective, and terrorism sting operations have a near-flawless record in court. If the government's terrorism stings were laid out on a time line, you'd see a slow start from 2002 to 2004 and then an explosion in 2005 and 2006. "Agents everywhere said, 'Hey, this worked in New York. Let's try it over here,'" Peter Ahearn, the former FBI agent, told me when I explained to him how the data showed that the terrorism stings spread nationwide from a modest start in Florida and New York. "That's nothing new in the FBI. You always look at what other agents are doing. What are they doing there that we can do here?"

If the only effective measure is based on court verdicts, then terrorism sting operations have become a proven product for the Bureau. And this product carries another benefit: a terrorism sting gives the FBI, under pressure to show results, something to hold up—a dangerous terrorist caught on tape, convicted at trial, sentenced to decades in prison—as evidence to the public that it is doing its job to safeguard the United States from another attack.

8.MISSION ACCOMPLISHED

Since the U.S. Congress sets the annual budget of the Federal Bureau of Investigation, the law enforcement priorities of the Bureau are, by necessity, political in nature. In fiscal year 2011–2012, the FBI allocated more than $3 billion of its $7.8 billion budget to counterterrorism. By comparison, the FBI's criminal division, responsible for investigating organized crime and financial fraud, among other areas, received $2.5 billion.[1] More than a decade after terrorists flew commercial airplanes into the World Trade Center and the Pentagon, preventing the next attack is still the number one priority for the FBI.

To justify its counterterrorism budget, the Bureau must demonstrate to both the public and elected officials that it is preventing would-be terrorists from taking aim at the homeland, just as in the 1980s and 1990s, the FBI needed to show that it was on top of the Mafia and drug runners. The best way to demonstrate a job well done is by citing investigations that are made public through prosecutions. But what if there haven't been many terrorists in the United States since 9/11? Or, alternatively, what if the FBI has created such a hostile environment for terrorists that none has dared strike since September 11, 2001? One of these could be true, since we haven't had a significant terrorist attack on U.S. soil since 9/11. The former would undermine the FBI's top priority, however, and the latter would give the FBI nothing to show to Congress to justify the money it receives for counterterrorism—no arrest and conviction numbers, no compelling narratives of deadly plots foiled.

Terrorism sting operations neatly solve this dilemma, and since 9/11, the Bureau has used them to great effect in demonstrating to Congress and the American public that it is "winning" the war on terrorism. In testimony before the Senate Judiciary Committee on January 20, 2010, FBI Director Robert Mueller specifically cited four terrorism sting cases, including the Newburgh case involving the hapless James Cromitie and his band of petty criminals, as evidence of the growing and changing terrorist threat in the United States. "This is merely a sampling of the investigations we have handled over the past year," Mueller said.[2] In fact, an extensive ten-year record exists of the FBI citing terrorism cases that seem very dangerous at first blush and then turn out to be anything but on closer inspection. Shortly after 9/11, for example, the FBI hotly pursued the so-called Lackawanna Six, a group of young Yemeni American friends living near Buffalo, New York, who had attended an Al Qaeda training camp in Afghanistan in the spring of 2001. The FBI at first portrayed the group as a sleeper cell, and in his State of the Union address on January 28, 2003, President George W. Bush mentioned the case, saying that, "We've broken Al Qaeda cells in Hamburg, London, Paris, as well as Buffalo, New York."[3] While it was true that members of the Lackawana Six had attended a training camp near Kandahar and one of the men reportedly met Osama bin Laden there, the only sleeper cell they could have formed would have been one in deep hibernation. In reality, the six men from Lackawanna, New York, all naturalized U.S. citizens, realized during their time at the camp that they had romanticized Al Qaeda and the terrorist life, and wanted nothing more than to return to the comforts of home. As proof of this, when the FBI was flying one of the Lackawanna Six back to the United States, the man's only question was uniquely American: "How are the Buffalo Bills doing?"[4] While the six men were convicted of providing material support to Al Qaeda, they have all since been released from prison, with the U.S. government giving three of them new identities upon their release.[5] Described as terrorists by President Bush in 2003, the Lackawanna Six are now living free in the United States. They could be your neighbors.

There are many more examples of the U.S. government's hyping terrorism cases. When the FBI and Justice Department first announced the arrests of the Liberty City Seven on June 23, 2006—a case that ultimately took three trials to win convictions against five of the seven men who, evidence showed, had no capacity to commit a crime were it not for an aggressive informant with a history of lying to government agents—the FBI held up the case as an example of how it was preventing the next deadly attack. "Today's indictment is an important step forward in the war on terrorism here in the United States," John Pistole, the FBI's deputy director at the time, declared proudly during a press conference in Washington, D.C., adding:

> As you know, the Department of Justice and the FBI's highest priority is preventing another terrorist attack. And thanks to the efforts of each agent and officer who worked on this investigation together, we identi-

fied and disrupted a terrorist plot before any harm could be done. The investigation reveals outstanding work by the law enforcement community. It also reminds us that we have much more work to do.[6]

However, it became obvious that the government was exaggerating the strength and credibility of the Liberty City Seven when, during the same press conference, then-U.S. Attorney General Alberto Gonzales told reporters: "These individuals wish to wage a, quote, 'full ground war' against the United States." Later, a reporter asked Gonzales if the group allegedly planning a ground war had any actual contacts with Al Qaeda. "The answer to that is no," he responded. The federal government was putting before cameras the equivalent of a perp walk—a made-for-TV show that wasn't hard to spot. At least it wasn't for comedian Jon Stewart, who pilloried the announcement on *The Daily Show* three days after the press conference. "Seven guys?" he said on June 26, 2006. "I am not a general. I am not in any way affiliated with a military academy, but I believe if you are going to wage a full ground war against the United States, you will need to field at least as many people as, say, a softball team."[7]

The government's playing up of terrorism cases, which even years ago had become the butt of late-night jokes from TV comedians, should be worn out today. But it isn't. Four years after the Liberty City Seven announcement, with a new president in the White House, the government put on the same show in announcing the arrest of Mohamed Osman Mohamud in Portland, Oregon. At first glance, the plot appeared to be dangerous and deadly, the government swooping in to stop a crazed terrorist from killing thousands during a Christmas tree lighting ceremony. As we have seen, Mohamud was an underachieving, penniless young man whose alleged act of terrorism was only made possible by the FBI.

Despite this, Mohamud's case has become a rallying point for the FBI. High-ranking agents I have interviewed consistently used the case as their prime example in defending terrorism sting operations. "Look at what the kid in Portland wanted to do," J. Stephen Tidwell, the retired executive assistant director of the FBI, told me a couple of months after Mohamud's arrest. Even as U.S. Muslim civil and religious rights groups including the Council on American-Islamic Relations and Muslim Advocates asked the government to reconsider the use of sting operations in the wake of the Mohamud case, the government remained steadfast in defense of its aggressive tactics. "Mr. Mohamud's arrest was the result of a successful undercover operation—a critical and frequently used law enforcement tool that has helped identify and defuse public safety threats such as those posed by potential terrorists, drug dealers, and child pornographers for decades," Attorney General Eric Holder said during a December 10, 2010, speech, less than two weeks after Mohamud's arrest.[8]

The Mohamud case was among the last in a run of terrorism stings that occurred in 2010. During a November 29, 2010, press conference, a reporter asked Attorney General Holder about these cases. "Some critics say that this is another case of entrapment by the FBI in these matters," the reporter began. "And I'm just wondering if you can address that and also discuss why these sting operations are so important at this time. This is, I think, about the fifth or sixth case—sting in the last year." Holder held firm to the government's line that sting cases do not result in entrapment and instead provide an effective means for identifying terrorists before they strike. "This is an investigation I have been familiar with throughout the course—throughout its course. And I am confident there is no entrapment here and no entrapment claim will prove to be successful," Holder said. The attorney general then continued:

> There were, as I said, a number of opportunities that the subject in this matter, the defendant in this matter, was given to retreat, to take a different path. He chose at every step to continue. Some of the things that were contained in the court filings that we made indicate, I think, his state of mind, where he was told that children, children, were potentially going to be harmed by what he planned to do in blowing up the Christmas tree. And you saw his response. These investigations are extremely important. It is part of a forward-leaning way in which the Justice Department, the FBI, our law enforcement partners at the state and local level are trying to find people who are bound and determined to harm Americans and American interests around the world.[9]

Just as the FBI and the Justice Department used sting operations and conviction numbers to demonstrate to Congress and the American public that federal law enforcement was winning the war on drugs in the 1980s and 1990s, agents and prosecutors today use terrorism stings to demonstrate the same about the war on terrorism. But the major difference—something that Holder and top officials at the Justice Department and FBI won't acknowledge—is that while decades of data suggests that someone interested in obtaining drugs will be able to buy drugs even if not caught in a government sting, no data supports the assumption that a would-be terrorist would find the means to commit a terrorist act if not preempted by an FBI sting. To date, there has not been a single would-be terrorist in the United States who has become operational through a chance meeting with someone able to provide the means for a terrorist attack. In addition, no evidence suggests that Al Qaeda-affiliated operatives are within the United States today, willing and able to provide weapons to terrorist wannabes. In truth, the only people providing these means are undercover FBI agents and their informants, who help create the terrorists the Bureau is given more than $3 billion every year to catch.

Michael German, who spent sixteen years with the FBI infiltrating white supremacist groups, told me that funding is among the clearest predictors of results in the FBI. Simply put, if you spend more money in a specific area, you'll get more results in that area. But that doesn't necessarily mean that the area you're focusing on was a problem in the first place. Now a senior policy counsel for the American Civil Liberties Union, German said the culture of the FBI is results-driven, so no matter the assignment, FBI agents can't come up empty. "You have an enormous amount of pressure to do something," German told me. "If you are the terrorism agent in a benign Midwestern city, and there is no terrorism problem, you don't get to say, 'There's no terrorism problem here.' You still have to have informants and produce some evidence you're doing something." While FBI and Justice Department officials won't concede this point, some rank-and-file agents do. Several have told me off the record that chasing terrorists is like chasing ghosts—you'll only see them if you're willing to let your eyes play tricks on you. This is something that active agents won't talk about on the record for fear of retribution, while most retired agents, with German and James Wedick among the few exceptions, remain silent due to a concern about burning bridges with former colleagues.

In the fall of 2011, however, we were offered a rare glimpse into an active agent's criticism of the FBI's focus on terrorism. A twenty-year Midwestern veteran of the Bureau retired, and on September 30, 2011, she sent an email to ten colleagues with the subject line "It'll never make the Investigator," referring to the FBI's internal magazine for employees.[10] The email itself was blank, but there was a Word document attached to it titled "Instigator." The agent who sent the email asked me not to reveal her name or the names of the email's recipients, but in the Word document, she described how the FBI had become "reborn as the red-headed stepchild of the intelligence community":

> The truth is, they could waterboard me and I still would not say that ... the whole intel-based model of how the Bureau is expected to operate is anything more than smoke and poorly aligned mirrors. Yet another irony is that after struggling for twenty years to develop quality sources, I finally succeeded, only to be told that I'm still a failure because although my sources provide timely, pertinent, actionable information about ongoing public corruption and money laundering, they know nothing of Somali pirates or Chinese hackers.

This email was forwarded around the Bureau. One agent wrote: "Gentleman, she said it better than I could/can/will." Inherent in the criticism is the belief that, as a result of focusing billions of dollars on terrorism, the FBI is missing other criminals who represent greater threats to the United

States than lone wolves with big mouths and inert bombs provided by informants. Just as the FBI's executives are under pressure from Congress and the White House to show that the Bureau is combating terrorism, field supervisors are under pressure from those executives, and in turn these supervisors pressure agents to develop sources and cases related to national security—not public corruption, money laundering, organized crime, and other traditional areas of investigation for the FBI.

This is a bureaucratic phenomenon more than anything. Since terrorism represents the FBI's best-funded area, agents bring in terrorism cases, as if on automatic pilot. Along these lines, if tomorrow the Bureau dedicated half of its resources to, say, Wyoming, the least populous state in the union would suddenly become a hotbed for crime and public corruption. Yet all the FBI agents stuck in Cheyenne and Casper would send out emails complaining about having to search for imaginary crooks in Wyoming when they're sitting on great tips about organized crime and public corruption in New York and Los Angeles.

But just as you'd expect FBI officials to have a sense of the level of crime and corruption in Wyoming—and realize that spending billions in the Cowboy State would be a colossal waste of federal law enforcement resources—you would think that the Bureau had at least preliminary information before 9/11 that suggested how supportive U.S. Muslim communities would be of foreign terrorist organizations and whether these communities were likely to harbor terrorists.

Retired FBI veteran Myron Fuller believes that none of the pre-9/11 intelligence suggested that Muslims in the United States were connected to international terrorist organizations or were supporting terrorists overseas, but that the Bureau chose to assume that that information was incorrect in the wake of the devastating terrorist attacks. In the late 1990s, Fuller was in charge of 200 FBI employees in 46 countries in Asia, including in Pakistan and Afghanistan, where he and his team uncovered information about Islamic militants who, intelligence suggested, were planning attacks in Europe. But his reports to the FBI's Washington headquarters, like those from pre-9/11 counterterrorism section chief John O'Neill, fell on deaf ears, and nothing came of his investigations, which Fuller thinks might have led to the 9/11 attackers had the FBI and CIA been willing to support his efforts.

Fuller retired from the Bureau just before 9/11 and now lives in Honolulu, where he's watched with a critical eye the evolution of the FBI's counterterrorism program. He said that the billions of dollars allocated to terrorism have forced the FBI to assume that a danger exists in communities where intelligence indicates no threat is present, and sting cases are simply the Bureau's way of justifying how it's spending all the money it receives for counterterrorism. Fuller is certainly in a position to know about this, since one of his responsibilities for the FBI in Asia was researching links between U.S. Muslim communities and international terrorist organizations. "We've been observing Muslim communities in the United States for thirty, forty years," Fuller told me when I talked to him a few months before the tenth anniversary of 9/11. "Until the '90s nothing developed from those operations that caused people to say we've got a threat here." Then came the first World Trade Center bombing in 1993. "Thereafter, we were taking a little bit stronger look at Muslim communities. Yet no one came out of that harder look. No match or link whatsoever from observing the people who lived in places like Dearborn, Michigan. Nothing ever came out of Dearborn or anywhere else that was remotely connected to the people who did what they did in 1993, or any of the attacks up to and including 9/11." Fuller added: "It's always been my argument that Muslim communities in the United States haven't been supporting terrorism or sheltering terrorists in any significant way. The response to 9/11 was to use a nuclear weapon to kill a gnat. People suddenly thought that if you're a Muslim, you're either a terrorist or a terrorist sympathizer."

With $3 billion directed at counterterrorism, the FBI can't come back to Congress and say, "We spent all the money, and the good news is that we didn't find any terrorists." Having a well-financed counterterrorism program means that the FBI must find terrorists to justify the program's existence, and terrorism sting operations provide a convenient and efficient means to show that a threat exists. However, the fact that there haven't been any terrorists who have been active members of U.S. Muslim communities, outside of those lured into stings, supports the assumption of former FBI agents like Myron Fuller that there aren't capable terrorists in those communities.

In using sting operations to pin up a "Mission Accomplished" banner in the war on terrorism, the FBI has had a powerful, if naïve, ally—the news media. Whenever the FBI announces a new terrorism sting, the media turns up the fear dial a notch, making it easy for the Bureau to demonstrate how it is ferreting out terrorists within the United States. For example, on September 25, 2009, ABC's *Good Morning America* woke up Americans with news that the FBI had apprehended a man who tried to set off a car bomb in the garage of Fountain Place, a sixty-story late modernist skyscraper in downtown Dallas. "The thousands of people inside the sixty-story skyscraper in downtown Dallas did not know it yesterday, but the

FBI says a man was outside, trying to kill as many of them as he could," reporter Pierre Thomas told television viewers that morning. "According to authorities, Hosam Smadi, an illegal immigrant from Jordan who had declared his love for Osama bin Laden, parked what he thought was a powerful car bomb in the tower's basement, his goal to, quote, 'bring down the building.' The FBI says Smadi eagerly dialed a cell phone to trigger the blast by remote."

The program then cut to a woman identified as Smadi's friend. "He babysat our kids. He, you know, if anybody needed anything, he was always there," she said. The show then went back to Thomas, who continued: "It was a sting. The explosives were fake. Smadi had been set up by the FBI, who learned of his alleged call for jihad on the Internet last March. The Bureau then laid a trap, introducing Smadi to a cell of operatives who were actually working for the FBI. His friends don't believe it."[11]

As with most reporting on FBI terrorism sting operations, everything in the Smadi story was front-loaded, with the media distributing unchallenged the government's narrative that Smadi was a dangerous terrorist, reinforcing the perception that a threat is out there and a terrorist could strike at any time. But what came out later in the Smadi case, well after the story was off the national broadcasts, was that the so-called terrorist was a twenty-year-old kid whom the FBI had discovered mouthing off on an online chat room for Muslim extremists. When Smadi first met with an undercover FBI agent as part of the sting, he wasn't interested in attacking the United States at all, but instead wanted to fight with the Taliban in Pakistan. Bombing a local target was actually the undercover agent's idea, and the FBI provided the fake bomb, the cell phone that was supposed to trigger that bomb, and everything else Smadi needed for the attack.[12] Viewers of *Good Morning America* on September 25, 2009, were left with the thought that the FBI had saved them from a would-be terrorist, when the truth was that the FBI had turned an angry young man caught ranting online into someone seemingly capable of causing mass destruction.

Nearly a year later, the media again offered unchallenged the government's view when the FBI and the Justice Department announced the arrest of Farooque Ahmed, a thirty-four-year-old Pakistani-born computer engineer who had plotted with undercover FBI agents to bomb the Metro system in Washington, D.C. Ahmed had provided drawings and information about Metro stations to people he believed were Al Qaeda operatives.[13] The bust made national news, once again fueling the perception that there were dangerous and capable terrorists in the United States. However, authorities were forced to admit that the public was never in any actual danger during the Ahmed sting. In a press conference for the Washington, D.C., news media, Michael Tabor, chief of the Metro Transit Police Department, explained that the would-be terrorist never had any opportunity to terrorize anyone. "Now I want to make myself perfectly clear that at no time were any patrons, employees, facilities associated with the Washington Area Metropolitan Transit System in jeopardy," Tabor said.[14]

Even when it comes to in-depth reporting, the traditional news media have been unwilling to cast a critical eye at terrorism sting operations. For an example of this, let's turn back again to the case of Antonio Martinez, the twenty-two-year-old Baltimore man who tried to bomb a military recruiting center. In January 2011, *Frontline* on PBS aired a collaborative story with the *Washington Post* documenting the enormous growth since 9/11 in the number of government contractors involved in the surveillance of U.S. citizens for counterterrorism purposes and how this industry is kept largely secret from the general public. Toward the end of the twenty-one-minute segment, *Frontline* attempted to show that despite our growing surveillance state, the terrorism cases we've heard about weren't thwarted by privacy-invading technology. One of the examples the program used was Martinez, who initially came to the government's attention after a private citizen reported his Facebook rants to the FBI. *Frontline* used the Martinez case to show that, despite all the investments in surveillance technology, none of it was used to catch this apparent terrorist.

"I'm trying to think of any other technology that would have helped in this case," reporter Dana Priest said in an interview with FBI Special Agent-in-Charge Richard McFeeley.

"This was good, old-fashioned police work by a lot of different police agencies coming together," McFeeley responded.

"Okay. So not so heavy on the technology," Priest said.

"That's correct," McFeeley said.

The point being made was that all this intrusive surveillance technology wasn't helpful in finding terrorists. But *Frontline* never questioned if someone such as Martinez, who was lured into an FBI sting by an aggressive informant, could legitimately even be considered a terrorist if he lacked the capacity to commit acts of terror on his own. Since the media have largely abdicated the role of defining who is and is not a terrorist to the FBI and Justice Department, the government has been able to push forward cases with no links to real terrorists and use the resulting publicity to demonstrate a terrorism-thwarting job seemingly well done.

In addition, without critical questioning from the media, or any kind of independent verifying organization, law enforcement is able to use its own data to create the narrative that dangerous terrorists are targeting us. For example, in March 2012, the New York City Police Department published a list of fourteen terrorism cases since 9/11 that the NYPD had seemingly prevented. A flattering June 2012 *Newsweek* profile of New York Police Commissioner Ray Kelly cited those fourteen cases, as did U.S. Representative Peter King, a New York Republican who held controversial congressional hearings on homegrown Islamic terrorists.[15] The problem with the NYPD's list was that only two of the cases involved real terrorists in New York—planned subway bomber Najibullah Zazi and failed Times Square bomber Faisal Shahzad—while another was a plot in the United Kingdom only tangentially linked to New York. The other eleven plots either never had credibility in the first place or involved FBI informants, such as the Newburgh Four and the Herald Square bombing plots. To justify its own success, the NYPD cited its own data, which is something the FBI has been doing with terrorism since 9/11—using data of its own creation to prove the point that terrorists are a growing threat that the Bureau is addressing.

Because the FBI has the luxury of determining alone who is and who is not a terrorist, simply by labeling them as such to the public, the government is able to create the very data by which its success can be measured. When the Justice Department asked Congress to allow prosecutors to put 9/11 mastermind Khalid Sheikh Mohammed on trial in Manhattan—a plan DOJ officials later scuttled for security reasons in favor of Guantanamo Bay as the venue—Attorney General Eric Holder provided congressional representatives with a list of more than 400 international terrorism-related defendants the Justice Department had prosecuted since 9/11. Holder provided this list as a way of showing that the DOJ had a near-flawless record in prosecuting terrorism defendants inside the United States, and thus was more than capable of putting Mohammed on trial. While the list did include one dangerous terrorist, Najibullah Zazi, as well as people who were raising money for or sending money to terrorist groups such as Hamas, the Tamil Tigers in Sri Lanka, and the Revolutionary Armed Forces of Colombia, others who made the list were terrorists only because the Justice Department had labeled them as such. The list included several sting targets whose terrorist acts were only made possible by the FBI, such as the five convicted members of the Liberty City Seven, Mohammed Hossain, and the Fort Dix Five. Other inclusions seemed arbitrary, if not deceitful. Amr I. Elgindy, an Egyptian-born stock trader who received confidential information from an FBI agent that he used to manipulate stock prices, was on the list, even though he had no connections to terrorism whatsoever and evidence showed that his motivation was greed, not religion or ideology. Also on the list were New Jersey men Hussein and Nasser Abuali and Rabi Ahmed, who were busted in a storeroom full of Kellogg's cereal worth nearly $90,000. No evidence linked them to terrorism, and they were never charged with a terrorism-related offense. "This case had no connection to terrorism unless you consider cornflakes weapons of mass destruction," Michael Pedicini, a lawyer for one of the men, said.[16] Yet the Justice Department was able to include the cereal bandits on a list of dangerous terrorists because no one independently audits the terrorist data by which the government is measuring itself.

Congress allocates billions to the FBI to find terrorists and prevent the next attack. The FBI in turn focuses thousands of agents and informants on Muslim communities in sting operations that pull easily influenced fringe members of these communities into terrorist plots conceived and financed by the FBI. The Justice Department then labels these targets, who have no capacity on their own to commit terrorist acts and no connections to actual terrorists, as terrorists and includes them in data intended not only to justify how previous dollars were spent, but also to justify the need for future counterterrorism funding. In the end, the tail wags the dog in a continual cycle.

9. ONE MAN'S TERRORIST, ANOTHER MAN'S FOOL

He sent the email in the middle of the night on March 9, 2012, and it went to dozens of people—journalists, lawyers, activists. The subject line read "Shahed Hussain." Khalifah Al-Akili, a thirty-four-year-old living near Pittsburgh, had found the article I'd written for *Mother Jones* about FBI informants, which detailed, among many things, Hussain's life and work with federal law enforcement. Al-Akili discovered while reading the article that his new friend "Mohammed," pictured alongside the text in my story, was one of the FBI's most prolific terrorism informants. What Al-Akili didn't know, however, was that the man who had introduced to him to Hussain was another one of the FBI's favorite informants, Theodore Shelby, the former Black Panther and tollbooth robber who had led the sting against Tarik Shah, the jazz-bassist-turned-terrorist from New York City.

In the email, Al-Akili said that he first met Shelby outside Jamil's Global Village, a store in Pittsburgh, in October 2011. As he had during the Shah investigation in New York, Shelby went by the name Saeed Torres. Al-Akili saw Shelby again at his mosque, An-Nur Islamic Center, in Wilkinsburg, Pennsylvania, where the informant told him that he lived just down the road from him, on Kelly Street. "He offered to ride me home when we was leaving, and I left with him," Al-Akili wrote. "Over time we continued to meet at the musjid for the prayer, and then he began to pick me up and take me to the musjid." Shelby told Al-Akili that he was interested in fighting and that he knew some people who had the means and desire to fund an attack. He also asked Al-Akili several times his opinions on jihad, which made Al-Akili wonder if Shelby was working for the FBI.

Later that month, Al-Akili told Shelby that he was going to Philadelphia for a few days. "I want you to see if you can get me a roscoe," Al-Akili remembered Shelby telling him, using an antiquated term for a gun. "I have some young boys selling drugs in front of my house, and I need some protection in case one of them gets out of hand." Al-Akili returned from Philadelphia three days later, and Shelby asked if he had the gun. No, Al-Akili told him, as he didn't "deal with brothers on that." Shelby continued to press. Did he know anyone in Pittsburgh who could get him a gun?

The agitation from Shelby never stopped. For example, when Al-Akili mentioned that he was interested in opening a Halal restaurant in Pittsburgh, Shelby told him he knew someone who could put up money for the eatery—but he'd need to do something in return. Al-Akili knew that "something" meant violence. "When he would talk like this, I would just remain silent for the most part and not really comment back," Al-Akili wrote in his email. He began trying to avoid Shelby, but he'd still end up running into him since the two lived so close to one another.

On January 15, 2012, Shelby told Al-Akili that he had a brother coming to town and that he wanted the two of them to meet. His brother was a man of the "struggle," to use Shelby's word, which he intended to mean jihad. When and where could they meet? The next day at one o'clock, Al-Akili told him. But after thinking about it, Al-Akili changed his mind. He sent a text message to Shelby, telling him that he had to cancel because he was going to see his ill mother.

A week passed, and on January 19, Al-Akili was walking to his apartment when he saw Shelby's truck and waved. Because of the truck's darkly tinted windows, Al-Akili couldn't see inside. The truck pulled up next to him, the passenger-side door opened, and a slender man of South Asian descent got out and approached. "*As-Salamu Alaykum*," the man said, kissing both of Al-Akili's cheeks. The man told Al-Akili his name was Mohammed, and that he'd been looking forward to meeting him. He'd heard so much about him, he said. Mohammed, as Al-Akili would later discover, was FBI serial snitch Shahed Hussain.

Hussain asked if they could have coffee together. Al-Akili declined, saying he had to go see his mother, who was ill. Shelby could drive him there, Hussain offered. Again Al-Akili declined, saying he'd take the bus. "So as they left, and as I was walking home, I had a feeling that I had just played out a part in some Hollywood movie where I had just been introduced to the leader of a terrorist sleeper cell," Al-Akili wrote.

Al-Akili told a friend, Dawud, about what had happened. As they were discussing the encounter in Al-Akili's apartment, the phone rang. Shelby and Hussain were on the line, and they were downstairs. Al-Akili told them he wasn't at home, a lie. "I just thought maybe you and Dawud might be upstairs just sitting around," Shelby said.

He wasn't home, Al-Akili told Shelby again.

"I really want to meet you, brother, and I have a card for your mother because she is not feeling good," Hussain said. Al-Akili knew then that he was being watched. The next morning, as he was walking down the street, Hussain turned the corner right in front of him. "As-Salamu Alaykum," he said, and asked again if they could have coffee together. There was a McDonald's nearby, so Al-Akili agreed.

Over coffee, Hussain told Al-Akili that he had an import business, the same story he had told Mohammed Hossain in Albany and James Cromitie in Newburgh. But with Al-Akili, Hussain didn't waste time with pleasantries. He said he was from Pakistan, near the border with Afghanistan, and that his people were in the business of jihad. "I hear you want to go to Pakistan," Hussain said.

"No, I don't want to go to Pakistan," Al-Akili replied. He then told Hussain he had to go, and asked the informant to write down his phone number, email address, and the name of his business. Hussain scribbled the information on a McDonald's receipt. "He kept attempting to talk about the fighting going on in Afghanistan, which I clearly felt was an attempt to get me to talk about my views or understanding of that matter," Al-Akili remembered.

When he got home that evening, Al-Akili pulled out the receipt and sat down at his computer. First, he Googled the business name Hussain had given him—Seagull Enterprises—but couldn't find anything relevant. He then Googled the phone number—518-522-2965—thinking that might bring up information about the business. But it didn't. Instead, the first search result was an FBI transcript of a recorded phone conversation between Hussain and James Cromitie on April 5, 2009, which had been entered into evidence in the Newburgh trial and posted online. Since the Newburgh investigation, the FBI had never bothered to change Hussain's phone number. Al-Akili then Googled "James Cromitie" and found a Wikipedia entry mentioning

Hussain as the informant in the case. Finally, Al-Akili Googled "Shahed Hussain," stumbled onto my *Mother Jones* article and the picture of Hussain, and realized that the man who said his name was Mohammed was in fact one of the FBI's most effective and productive terrorism agent sprovocateurs. "I would like to pursue a legal action against the FBI due to their continuous harassment and attempts to set me up," Al-Akili wrote in his email. "This is just the latest attempt of the FBI to entrap me in their game of cat-and-mouse."

I wrote back to Al-Akili, and we arranged a time to talk by phone. But our conversation never happened, as less than a week after Al-Akili sent his email message, federal agents arrested him, charging him with being a felon in possession of a firearm. (Al-Akili, whose former name is James Marvin Thomas Jr., had pleaded guilty to two felony drug charges in 2001.) Included in the government's evidence against Al-Akili, which the FBI disclosed in its affidavit to commence prosecution, was an email from July 4, 2010, with an attached photo and links to two short YouTube videos, which have since been taken offline. In the photo and in the videos, Al-Akili is seen holding a .22-caliber rifle—a gun that wasn't his in 2010 and wasn't in his possession when he was arrested nearly two years later. A federal judge ordered Al-Akili to be held without bond pending trial after FBI Special Agent Joseph Bieshelt testified that Al-Akili had told an FBI informant he planned to travel to Pakistan and fight with the Taliban.[1] He has pleaded not guilty and is awaiting trial.

The charges against Khalifah Al-Akili were the culmination of the FBI's latest sting operation involving Shahed Hussain, an accused murderer and con artist who in less than ten years has become one of the Bureau's most valuable terrorism informants. The Al-Akili sting offers a window into how far the FBI is willing to go to create the very terrorists it's charged with hunting. Given his previous drug charges, Al-Akili isn't the nation's best, most productive citizen, to be sure. But is he a potentially dangerous terrorist? An informant offered him money, and Al-Akili wouldn't buy a gun. In addition, Al-Akili was never in touch with terrorists in the United States or abroad. The only evidence linking him to terrorism is an unsubstantiated claim by the FBI that Al-Akili told an informant he wanted to fight with the Taliban—an imagined crime at best, if it's even true. Yet the FBI deemed this ex-con and convert to Islam so dangerous that agents assigned two of their most prolific and aggressive terrorism informants—men with histories of violence and fraud—to target him. When Al-Akili realized he was at the center of a setup, he sent an email nationwide sounding the alarm—not exactly the type of stealth behavior one would expect from a hardened lone wolf intent on wreaking havoc and carnage in America. After the sting operation was blown, the FBI arrested Al-Akili, labeled him a terrorist based on a comment he allegedly made to an informant with a record of lying, and prosecuted him using evidence from a two-year-old YouTube video clip in which he is seen holding a firearm.

Since 9/11, the FBI has routinely labeled men like Khalifah Al-Akili as terrorists, despite the lack of evidence that these men would commit terrorist acts without the aggressive prodding and assistance of FBI informants. (In Al-Akili's case, even the persistence of the informant was insufficient to push him into going along with a terrorist plot.) Part of the reason that the FBI is able to get away with this is because the public and the media don't question whether the individuals the Bureau puts on display are real terrorists or just men on the margins made to look like terrorists. Even when the government is clearly putting on a show, neither the public nor the mainstream media have stopped it. In the prosecution in Houston of a man who worked with a person he believed was an Al Qaeda trainer, for example, the federal government put on the witness stand an informant wearing a black mask, telling the judge that the mask was necessary because showing the informant's face could make him a target for terrorists.[2] No one pointed out that since actual terrorists weren't involved in the investigation, no real terrorists existed who would want to target the informant.

For the FBI, terrorism sting operations net results, and results confirm to the Bureau that a problem or threat exists, thereby supporting the belief that more terrorism sting operations are needed. While this type of cycle could be created from any kind of crime and with any law enforcement agency, it is hard to imagine that the public would tolerate widespread sting operations and aggressive informants used in anything other than terrorism investigations in Muslim communities. Imagine, for example, if law enforcement sent informants and undercover officers into poor minority communities in South Los Angeles and offered cash for stolen cars—and then used the resulting rash of arrests to prove how well the police were curbing the growing problem of auto theft, a problem the police had created in the first place. Would the public, alerted by African American and Hispanic community leaders to what would appear to be entrapment and racial and ethnic targeting, tolerate such behavior from law enforcement? The answer is no. Yet since 9/11, leaders in Muslim communities nationwide have objected to the FBI tactics used against their people, without any kind of support from the public or the media. I can only believe that the public either does not understand how egregious the FBI's practices are, or believes that keeping the United States safe from would-be terrorists justifies limits to justice and civil rights for a single minority group.

To this day, the FBI continues to manufacture terrorism crimes in Muslim communities. By not challenging the FBI and the Justice Department, the public and the media have tacitly condoned sting operations against men with no capacity on their own to commit serious crimes. If the FBI's top priority is to find and stop lone wolves, and these lone wolves are found only through FBI stings that border on entrapment and target easily influenced men with financial troubles or mental problems, providing the FBI with a deep pool of potential terrorists, then how will the Bureau ever know when terrorism is no longer a threat, and the time has come to shift priorities?

I asked Arthur Cummings, the former executive assistant director of the FBI's National Security Branch and one of the most ardent supporters of terrorism stings, about this. What I needed to understand, he told me, was that the FBI's true enemies weren't so much Al Qaeda and Islamic terrorism but rather the idea of Al Qaeda and Islamic terrorism. It was November 2010, and the Justice Department had in the previous couple of months announced a series of informant-led terrorism sting cases, which included plots to bomb Wrigley Field in Chicago and the Metro system in Washington, D.C. Cummings had retired from the Bureau a few months before the government announced these cases. We met at Southport Brewing Company in Connecticut, about a ninety-minute train ride from Manhattan. Cummings wore jeans and a light sweater and was drinking a pint of beer.

"We're at war with an idea," Cummings told me emphatically.

"But you can't kill an idea, can you?" I asked him.

"No," he replied.

"So that means this indefinite war, with terrorism stings, is something we'll live with for decades?"

"That's right," Cummings said.

When Barack Obama took office in January 2009, his administration provided some early indication that federal law enforcement would deemphasize the targeting of potential terrorists in Muslim communities and focus more attention on right-wing extremists and other growing threats in the United States. In April 2009, the Department of Homeland Security's Office of Intelligence and Analysis released a report titled "Rightwing Extremism: Current Economic and Political Climate Fueling Resurgence in Radicalization and Recruitment," warning that violence could come from right-wing extremists concerned about illegal immigration, abortion, increasing federal powers, and gun control.[3] Returning military veterans were particularly susceptible to recruitment into these extremist groups, the report said.

A political storm gathered following the report, with Fox News providing inspiration with exaggerated interpretations such as: "The government considers you a terrorist threat if you oppose abortion, own a gun, or are a returning war veteran."[4] U.S. Representative Lamar Smith, a Republican from Texas, accused the DHS of "political profiling." A House Homeland Security Committee inquiry followed, which the committee's then-chairman, Bennie Thompson, a Democrat from Mississippi, called "a GOP stunt aimed at embarrassing the new administration." In fairness, three months before the right-wing report, DHS had released an assessment predicting increased cyber threats from left-wing extremists—but the federal government's concerns about extremists on both ends of the political spectrum were cut out of the controversy, which became so great that Homeland Security Secretary Janet Napolitano withdrew the right-wing report and ordered it rewritten.

As a result, aggressively investigating right-wing extremism—a real threat in this country—became politically difficult, if not impossible, for the Obama administration. And so FBI investigations of perceived Islamic terrorists, and, to a much lesser extent, left-wing extremists, only increased. But then a deadly shooting in Arkansas—involving a right-wing domestic terrorist that the FBI had been monitoring but whose violence the Bureau chose not to preempt—forced the federal government to rethink some of its law enforcement priorities.

On May 20, 2010, at 11:36 a.m., Bill Evans, a police officer in West Memphis, Arkansas, stopped a white Dodge Caravan with Ohio plates that was traveling east on Interstate 40. Sgt. Brandon Paudert, whose father was the chief of police in this city of 26,245, arrived as backup. Evans suspected the car might be involved in drug trafficking. West Memphis is at the intersection of Interstates 40 and 55, which cross the country east-west and north-south, respectively, and for that reason, police there are wary of suspicious vehicles that may be moving drugs across the country.

Evans approached the white minivan and found forty-five-year-old Jerry R. Kane in the driver's seat. A white man with short-cropped brown hair, a beard, and a large belly, Kane wore a white T-shirt and blue jeans. Next to Kane was his sixteen-year-old son, Joseph. Evans asked Jerry Kane to get out of the vehicle, and the two men walked to the rear of the minivan. A dashboard camera in the black police SUV recorded the scene, though there was no audio.[5] Evans and Kane appeared to argue, and at one point, Kane pointed to his Ohio plates. Evans, seemingly unconvinced by whatever Kane was saying, decided to arrest the man and began to frisk him. That's when sixteen-year-old Joseph emerged from the passenger side of the minivan holding a Yugoslavian-manufactured AK-47 assault rifle. Evans placed one hand on his gun and another toward the boy, palm out, as if to say, "Stop." Kane opened fire, hitting Evans multiple times. Seeing his fellow officer gunned down, Paudert retreated behind the police vehicle for cover, pulled out his handgun, and fired several times at the teenage gunman, missing each time. But Paudert was in a weak tactical position, as his police-issued handgun was no match for the much more powerful assault rifle. Joseph Kane returned fire with the AK-47, and the ricocheting bullets struck Paudert in the head. The boy then ran back to the minivan. Evans was in the ditch, facedown and bleeding from multiple bullet wounds. Joseph opened fire again on the officer and then hopped into the minivan. He and his father sped off. A package delivery driver, passing by the shooting as it occurred, called 911.[6] "Officers down!" the call went out over the police radio.

Local police tracked the minivan to a nearby Walmart, where the Kanes had stopped to remove the Ohio license plate. The first to see the van was an Arkansas wildlife officer who heard the emergency call on the radio. He rammed his truck into the minivan to prevent the Kanes from getting away. A gun battle then ensued between the West Memphis police and the Kanes. Father and son were both killed.

Bob Paudert, the West Memphis chief of police, soon arrived at the stretch of road where two of his officers—one of them his son—had been shot. Paudert's wife was with him.

"Stay in the truck," he told her. "Don't get out."[7] Brandon Paudert, thirty-nine years old, had been struck eleven times by the high-powered assault rifle and was pronounced dead at the scene. Evans, thirty-seven years old, had been shot fourteen times and died later at the hospital.

The FBI was already there as Bob Paudert tried to take in what had happened. "We know who they are," Paudert remembered one of the FBI agents telling him. "They're domestic terrorists." A former long-haul trucker with fervent antigovernment beliefs, Kane at the height of the nationwide foreclosure crisis scratched out a living giving seminars in small hotel rooms that purported to teach distressed homeowners how they could not only save their homes from foreclosure, but also cancel out their mortgage obligations altogether. He steadily built a fringe following among tax protestors, conspiracy theorists, and people who believed the U.S. government was somehow illegitimate and did not have legal authority over them.

Kane followed a right-wing conspiracy theory known as redemption—a set of beliefs held by many members of the so-called sovereign citizen movement. Redemption theorists believe the U.S. government is a corporation that disguises commercial contracts as laws. By filing the appropriate paperwork with a county register, they believe, they can opt out of society's laws. Kane's foreclosure-avoidance techniques centered on filing inconsequential documents with the county recording office, which at best muck up the system and slow the pace of bureaucracy, providing temporary illusions of success when, for example, a foreclosure proceeding is delayed because the court needs time to sort through the bogus filings. Sovereign citizens, estimated to number more than 300,000 in the United States, are dangerous for law enforcement officers because they are typically well armed and something as a simple as a traffic stop can feed into their paranoid beliefs that government agents are persecuting them.

This paranoia was exemplified in a seminar Kane gave in California during which an attendee asked him what he could do about an aggressive state revenue agent. Kane suggested that violence was a solution, describing how he felt under constant threat from the government. "I don't want to have to kill anybody. But if they keep messing with me, that's what it's going to come down to," Kane said. "And if I have to kill one, then I'm not going to be able to stop. I just know it." A few months after that statement, despite having been tracked by the FBI since 2004 as possible domestic terrorists, Jerry and Joseph Kane murdered two law enforcement officers before dying in a gun battle with police. The bloodbath, which made international news, was something of a wake-up call for the FBI. An Ohio sheriff had warned the Bureau years earlier that he believed Kane was dangerous, and by the time the West Memphis shootings occurred, the FBI had built a substantial case file on Kane and his network of supporters—yet agents chose neither to act nor to share the information with local law enforcement in communities through which Kane and his son traveled.[8] "The FBI has focused so much on international terrorists and spent so much time training local law enforcement about how to spot international terrorists that they allowed domestic terrorists to stay under the radar without sharing information with locals," Bob Paudert, the West Memphis police chief who lost his son in the Kane shooting, told me when I talked to him two years after the killings. "What the West Memphis case brought to light was how we and most officers around the country had never heard of the sovereign citizen movement. The FBI knew about it—they had these guys in their database. But they never shared that information with us."

Paudert, now retired from the West Memphis Police Department, has lobbied the Justice Department to focus greater resources on right-wing domestic terrorists. He also travels the country providing training to local law enforcement officers on how to spot members of the sovereign citizen movement. He often hears complaints from local cops that the FBI wants them to focus on ferreting out Islamic terrorists when they are much more concerned about domestic threats. "They got zero training on domestic terrorists," Paudert said. "Everything from the FBI and DOJ was catered to international terrorists—what to look for, how they might act. Nothing was ever discussed about domestic terrorists. I think the FBI has done a superb job protecting our borders. But they've done a lousy job internally. I think the most serious national security threat to us today is domestic terrorists. These people—and I say this in my talks every time I give one—they are no different than international terrorists. They are so committed to their cause they are willing to die for it. They are willing to kill and be killed. That was evident in the Kanes' case. They were willing to die for their beliefs." In September 2011, citing the West Memphis shooting, the FBI formally recognized the sovereign citizen movement as a "growing domestic threat."[9]

If the FBI could miss—or ignore—something like the sovereign citizen movement, what else has it missed or ignored in the years since 9/11, being so hyper-focused on terrorism in Muslim communities? While cataloging missed opportunities is something of an exercise in speculation, there were enough major crimes over the decade that went unnoticed by federal law enforcement until it was too late to give credibility to that question. Main Street mortgage fraud and Wall Street financial fraud—which together created an economic toxin that pushed the United States into the worst recession since the Great Depression—were among the Bureau's areas of focus prior to 9/11.[10] So were financial Ponzi schemes, and in the decade that the FBI has kept one eye trained on terrorism, con men such as Bernie Madoff and R. Allen Stanford flourished, scamming away a total of more than $10 billion from investors.[11] If the FBI had not been so obsessed with stopping a terrorist attack that never came, and creating "terrorists," could they have stopped mortgage and Wall Street fraud before it spread globally like an uncontrollable contagion? Could FBI agents have taken down Ponzi artists before unsuspecting investors lost billions? Could agents have uncovered any number of crimes we have yet to hear of?

These are unanswerable questions. But as I researched terrorism sting operations and talked with current and former FBI agents who complained that in terrorism stings the government was creating bogeymen from buffoons, I've thought a lot about these questions, which remind me of a line that Peter Ahearn, the retired FBI agent who directed the Western New York Joint Terrorism Task Force and oversaw the investigation of the Lackawanna Six, offered when we sat in a coffee shop in the Washington, D.C., suburbs. "If you concentrate more people on a problem," Ahearn told me, "you'll find more problems." The corollary to that, of course, is that if you concentrate fewer people on a problem, you'll find fewer problems. It's conceivable that had the FBI not been chasing terrorists of its own creation, federal agents might have had the resources to prevent the financial crimes that ultimately brought the world economy to the brink of collapse—or stopped the sovereign citizen movement before men like Brandon Paudert were killed. However, since the U.S. Congress continues to mandate that the FBI focus on terrorism, and the FBI in turn churns out Islamic terrorism cases to prove that it is responsive to that mandate, it's conceivable that the Bureau will not notice or arrive too late to address the real crimes and threats of tomorrow.

The FBI currently spends $3 billion annually to hunt an enemy that is largely of its own creation. Evidence in dozens of terrorism cases—involving plots to blow up synagogues, skyscrapers, military recruiting stations, and bars and nightclubs—suggests that today's terrorists in the United States are nothing more than FBI creations, impressionable men living on the edges of society who become bomb-triggering would-be killers only because of the actions of FBI informants. The FBI and the Justice Department then cite these sting cases as proof that the government is stopping terrorists before they strike. But the evidence available for review in these cases shows that these "terrorists" never had the capability to launch an attack themselves. Most of the targets in these stings were poor, uneducated, and easily manipulated. In many cases, it's likely they wouldn't have come up with the idea at all without prodding by one of the FBI's 15,000 registered informants. In sting after sting, from Miami to Seattle, the FBI and its informants have provided the means for America's would-be terrorists to carry out an attack, creating what a federal judge has called a "fantasy terror operation."[12]

According to government and federal court records, the Justice Department has prosecuted more than 500 terrorism defendants since 9/11. Of these cases, only a few posed actual threats to people or property such as: Hesham Mohamed

Hadayet, who opened fire on the El Al ticket counter at Los Angeles International Airport on July 4, 2002; Najibullah Zazi, who came close to bombing the New York City subway system in September 2009; and Faisal Shahzad, who failed to detonate a car bomb in Times Square on May 1, 2010.[13] Of the rest of the approximately 500 defendants, more than 150 were caught conspiring not with terrorists but with FBI informants in sting operations. The remainder of the Justice Department's post-9/11 terrorism prosecutions involved crimes such as money laundering or immigration violations in which the link to terrorism was tangential or on another continent, and no evidence in these cases suggested credible safety threats to the United States.

The men the FBI and the Justice Department describe today as terrorists—among them Narseal Batiste, James Cromitie, Dritan Duka, Michael Finton, Hamid Hayat, Mohammed Hossain, Imran Mandhai, Antonio Martinez, Mohamad Osman Mohamud, Walli Mujahidh, Tarik Shah, and Derrick Shareef—may technically be terrorists under the law, as they have been convicted on terrorism-related charges in federal courts. But if they are indeed terrorists, the government has stretched the definition of a terrorist well beyond its limits. These men, some broke, others with mental problems, couldn't have committed even small-time offenses on their own, and yet the FBI and Justice Department have convinced courts and the public that they *are* terrorists, even though it was government informants and agents who provided the plans and weapons that allowed them to become terrorists in the first place.

The definition of who is and who isn't a terrorist has been a source of debate for more than 150 years. John Brown, an abolitionist who turned to violence in an attempt to free slaves in the South, raided Harpers Ferry Armory in West Virginia in 1859 for his cause. Southerners viewed Brown as a terrorist when he was executed, while many in the North saw Brown as a man forced to militancy in order to fight the violent enslavement of blacks in the agricultural South. To this day, historians and criminologists disagree over whether Brown was America's first terrorist.[14] Indeed, the definition of a terrorist depends largely on the person or institution defining it. Menachem Begin led the resistance against the British occupation of what became Israel, while Nelson Mandela was a militant who fought the apartheid government in South Africa. Both men, winners of the Nobel Peace Prize, are remembered today as statesmen—but they were once considered terrorists. Whether the Irish Republican Army or the Tamil Tigers were terrorists or revolutionaries depends on whose definition of terrorist you choose to adopt.

There's a famous saying—first used in Gerald Seymour's 1975 novel about the IRA, *Harry's Game*—that alludes to how the definition of a terrorist can be so loose and imprecise as to be form-fitting for the user of the word: "One man's terrorist is another man's freedom fighter." The saying is so often used, it's become a cliché. But I don't think this well-worn maxim can be used any longer, once you take a close look at the terrorism cases that have moved through federal courts in the years after 9/11. No one could think former crack cocaine addict James Cromitie, lured into a terrorist plot by the prospect of money, was a freedom fighter, or the young and disgruntled Antonio Martinez, who had trouble driving a car, a revolutionary. Like all FBI terrorism sting targets Cromitie and Martinez were dupes. Today, we need a new saying. One man's terrorist is another man's fool.

ACKNOWLEDGMENTS

During the course of researching FBI informants and terrorism sting operations, I received financial support from the Investigative Reporting Program at the University of California Berkeley, the Fund for Investigative Journalism, and the Carnegie Legal Reporting Fellowship at Syracuse University. Without the generous support of these institutions, I could not have written this book.

The Terror Factory: Inside the FBI's Manufactured War on Terrorism is an outgrowth of my work as a fellow at the Investigative Reporting Program at the University of California Berkeley, and for that reason, I owe thanks to Lowell Bergman, who runs the Investigative Reporting Program, for investing in my research, for his editorial guidance, and for helping me build sources within the Federal Bureau of Investigation. I'm grateful as well to *Mother Jones* and editor Monika Bauerlein for devoting a magazine cover and substantial resources to publish "The Informants," the magazine story that this book expands on, and help me build a database of terrorism prosecution since 9/11 that earned industry praise and won the prestigious Data Journalism Award. I also want to acknowledge *Miami New Times* editor, Chuck Strouse, who published a 2009 story I wrote about the FBI's coercion of a South Florida imam—a story that forms the basis of Chapter 4 and ultimately inspired me to spend more than a year analyzing how the Bureau recruits informants through coercion and then uses those informants in terrorism sting operations.

I don't suspect the transition from newspapers and magazines to books is ever comfortable and seamless one for journalists; it wasn't for me. But having Robert Lasner of Ig Publishing on the other side of every draft gave me confidence where I otherwise would have had anxiety. He and Elizabeth Clementson of Ig Publishing have my gratitude for seeing the book that was to be written from my reporting and then helping me shape that reporting into the work you've read today.

The backbone of my research for this book was a close and careful analysis of the prosecutions of more than 500 terrorism defendants since September 11, 2001. This required spending months pouring through court records from federal courthouses across the country. I could not have done this laborious research were it not for Lauren Ellis, a researcher at the Investigative Reporting Program who shared my intense curiosity about the people our Justice Department describes as terrorists today. Lauren developed a familiarity with more than 500 terrorism defendants and an expertise of many of them, and I am grateful for the hundreds of hours she spent helping me gather documents and analyze Justice Department terrorism cases in a systematic way.

Other researchers helped me along the way as well. Hamed Aleaziz, a former editorial fellow at *Mother Jones*, was a tenacious fact-checker who skillfully challenged some of my reporting and conclusions. Alexandra Kish and Brandie Middlekauff contributed research memoranda about specific cases and helped me understand how those cases fit into the specific themes I explored in this book.

I wrote *The Terror Factory* while working full-time at the Florida Center for Investigative Reporting, a Miami-based nonprofit that produces investigative journalism about Florida and Latin America in partnership with traditional print and broadcast media. For that reason, I owe my colleagues at FCIR, including Sharon Rosenhause and Mc Nelly Torres, thanks for their support of my outside interests, including this book. Sharon deserves additional thanks for the valuable feedback she offered on drafts of *The Terror Factory*.

Finally, none of my research would have been possible without help and cooperation from dozens of current and former FBI agents around the country. Some talked to me on a regular basis to help me determine what was happening in the Bureau as the Justice Department brought more than 500 alleged terrorists into U.S. District Courts in the decade after 9/11. Others alerted me to specific cases or provided documents that I otherwise would have been unable to obtain. Most of these FBI officials cannot be named here. But you know who you are, and truly, you have my sincerest gratitude.

NOTES

INTRODUCTION

1. "Feds: Al Qaeda Suspect May Not Be Threat at All," *Associated Press*, February 16, 2006.

2. Alfred Lubrano and John Shiffman, "Federal authorities Say W-B Man Is a Terrorist," *Philadelphia Inquirer*, February 12, 2006.

3. Indictment, United States v. Michael Curtis Reynolds, Oct. 3, 2006, http://theterrorfactory.com/documents/reynolds_ indictment.pdf.

1. TERROR TRAPS

1. Don Markus and Andrea F. Siegel, "Man Accused in Bomb Plot Had Prior Criminal Charges," *Baltimore Sun*, December 10, 2010.

2. Ibid.

3. Tricia Bishop, "Would-be Catonsville Bomber Sentenced to 25 Years in Prison," *Baltimore Sun*, April 6, 2012.

4. Criminal complaint, United States v. Antonio Martinez, December 8, 2010, http://theterrorfactory.com/documents/ martinez_complaint.pdf.

5. Ibid.

6. Ben Nuckols, "Lawyer: FBI entrapped Baltimore bomb plot suspect," *Associated Press*, December 13, 2010.

7. Ibid.

8. "Maryland Man Pleads Guilty to Attempted Use of a Weapon of Mass Destruction in Plot to Attack Armed Forces Recruiting Center," Federal Bureau of Investigation, 2012, http:// theterrorfactory.com/documents/FBI-Martinez.pdf.

9. *Inspire*, no.2, http://theterrorfactory.com/documents/inspire-

magazine-2.pdf.

10. *Inspire*, no.5, http://theterrorfactory.com/documents/inspire-magazine-5.pdf.

11. "Awlaki Video Urges U.S. Muslims to Join Al Qaeda," *Reuters*, December 20, 2011.

12. Patrik Jonsson and Tracey D. Samuelson, "Fort Hood Suspect: Portrait of a Terrorist?" *Christian Science Monitor*, November 9, 2009.

13. "Stats and Facts," Drug Enforcement Administration, 2011, http://www.justice.gov/dea/statistics.html#seizures.

14. Review the data cited here: http://theterrorfactory.com/database.html.

15. Rick Lyman and Nick Madigan, "Officials Puzzled About Motive of Airport Gunman Who Killed 2," *New York Times*, July 6, 2002.

16. William K. Rashbaum, "Terror Suspect Is Charged with Preparing Explosives," *New York Times*, September 25, 2009.

17. William K. Rashbaum, Mark Mazzetti, and Peter Baker, "Owner of S.U.V. Arrested in Times Sq. Bomb Case," *New York Times*, May 4, 2010.

18. Ethan Brown, *Snitch: Informants, Cooperators and the Corruption of Justice*, (New York: PublicAffairs, 2007).

19. Criminal complaint, United States v. Shahawar Matin Siraj, February 9, 2005, http://theterrorfactory.com/documents/siraj_complaint.pdf.

20. Author interview with Martin Stolar, 2011.

21. Review the data cited here: http://theterrorfactory.com/database.html.

22. Liz Kowalczyk, "*New York Times* Editor Chides White House," *Boston Globe*, June 17, 2012.

23. Donna Cassata, "Obama Security Record Gives GOP Few Openings," *Associated Press*, June 19, 2012.

24. "Attorney General Eric Holder Speaks at the Muslim Advocates' Annual Dinner," Department of Justice, December 10, 2010, http://theterrorfactory.com/documents/HolderSpeechDec2010.pdf.

2. THE NEW FBI

1. Michael Kirk and Jim Gilmore, "The Man Who Knew," PBS

Frontline, October 3, 2002.

2. Ibid.

3. Bassem Youssef v. Federal Bureau of Investigations, Deposition of Dale Watson, December 8, 2004.

4. Ibid.

5.

6. Author interview with Ali Soufan, 2011.

7. National Commission on Terrorist Attacks Upon the United States, "Final Report of the National Commission on Terrorist Attacks Upon the United States," July 22, 2004, http://theterrorfactory.com/documents/911Report.pdf.

8. Bassem Youssef v. Federal Bureau of Investigations, Deposition of Pasquale J. D'Amuro, November 30, 2004.

9. Ibid.

10. Bassem Youssef v. Federal Bureau of Investigations, Deposition of Arthur M. Cummings, II, March 14, 2005.

11. Ibid.

12. Ibid.

13. "CaseMap Facts Report," FBI document, January 8, 2010, http://theterrorfactory.com/documents/harrington_interview.pdf.

14. Cummings deposition.

15. Ibid.

16. Federal Bureau of Investigation, "Domestic Investigations and Operations Guide," December 16, 2008, http://theterrorfactory.com/documents/diog.pdf.

17. Federal Bureau of Investigation, "Domestic Investigations and Operations Guide," October 15, 2011, http://theterrorfactory.com/documents/diog2011.pdf.

18. Author interview with Arthur Cummings, 2010.

19. Ronald J. Ostrow and Robert L. Jackson, "U.S. Agents Make Increasing Use of Informants: But 'Handlers' Face Complex Legal Hazards When Condoning Criminal Acts," *Los Angeles Times*, June 15, 1986.

20. Dina Temple-Raston, "New FBI Computer Surveys Confidential Informants," *NPR*, July 11, 2007.

21. Author interview with Peter Ahearn, 2011.

22. Eric Lichtblau, "Threats and Responses: The Former F.B.I.

Director; Tough Security Questions Are Likely for Ex-Chief of F.B.I.," *New York Times*, April 13, 2004.

23. Author interview with Dale Watson, 2011.

24. Scott Shane and Lowell Bergman, "F.B.I. Struggling to Reinvent Itself to Fight Terror," *New York Times*, October 10, 2006.

25. Ibid.

26. Federal Bureau of Investigation, Memorandum, March 3, 2008, http://theterrorfactory.com/documents/ACLURM011160.pdf.

27. Federal Bureau of Investigation, Memorandum, May 11, 2007, http://theterrorfactory.com/documents/ACLURM012669.pdf.

28. Federal Bureau of Investigation, "The Baddest Town in America—and the FBI Owns It," http://www.fbi.gov/about-us/training/hogans-alley.

29. Spencer Ackerman, "FBI Teaches Agents: 'Mainstream' Muslims Are 'Violent, Radical,'" *Wired*, September 14, 2011.

30. Yassir Fazaga v. Federal Bureau of Investigation, Complaint, February 22, 2011, http://theterrorfactory.com/documents/CAIR-ACLU_Lawsuit.pdf.

3. MOHAMMED AND HOWARD

1. Jonathan Eig, *Get Capone: The Secret Plot yhat Captured America's Most Wanted Gangster* (New York: Simon & Schuster, 2010); Marc Perrusquia, "Photographer Ernest Withers Doubled as FBI Informant to Spy on Civil Rights Movement," *Commercial Appeal*, September 12, 2010.

2. Tanya Weinberg and Jeff Shields, "Informant's Role Central in Terrorism Case," *Sun-Sentinel*, June 12, 2002.

3. United States v. Narseal Batiste, "Narseal Batiste's Supplement to Demand for Specific Kyles and Brady Information and Giglio/Napue Materials and Request for Expedited Ruling," August 27, 2007, http://theterrorfactory.com/documents/batiste398main.pdf.

4. Ronald J. Ostrow, "Webster Chosen as CIA Director: President Picks FBI Chief to Head Agency Under Fire for Iran Role," *Los Angeles Times*, March 4, 1987.

5. Author interview with Stephen S. Trott, 2011.

6. David Kidwell and Larry Lebowitz, "FBI Sees Terror; Family Sees Good Son Ex-resident of Miramar Being Sought in Terror Case," *Miami Herald*, March 31, 2003.

7. Manuel Roig-Franzia and Dan Eggen, "From Bookish Boy to Focus of FBI Manhunt; Terror Suspect Labeled Worst Threat to U.S.," *Washington Post*, April 14, 2003.

8. Ibid.

9. Miami-Dade Police Department, Incident report, April 6, 2001, http://theterrorfactory.com/documents/assaad.pdf.

10. Alfonso Chardy, Juan O. Tamayo, and Jay Weaver, "10 Years After 9/11, Suspected Al-Qaida Figure Still Eludes FBI," *McClatchy-Tribune News Service*, August 31, 2011.

11. Tracy Breton, "Fear of Terrorists Haunted FBI Informant," *Providence Journal-Bulletin*, January 26, 2003.

12. Ibid.

13. Eric Lichtblau and James Risen, "Bank Data Is Sifted by U.S. in Secret to Block Terror," *New York Times*, June 23, 2006.

14. Author interview with Max Rameau, 2009.

15. Chuck Strouse, "Penniless Purgatory," *Miami New Times*, October 26, 2006.

16. John O'Neil, "Terror Plot Was in 'Earliest Stages,' Gonzales Says," *New York Times*, June 23, 2006.

17. Doug Simpson, "Terror Suspect Grew Up in Christian Family," *Associated Press*, June 26, 2006.

18. Doug Simpson, "Father: Sears Tower Plot Suspect Not in 'Right Mind,'" *Associated Press*, June 25, 2006.

19. Adam Goldman and Matt Apuzzo, "NYPD Docs: 'Focus' scrutiny on Muslim Americans," March 9, 2012.

20. Miami Beach Police Department, Incident report, November 10, 2004, http://theterrorfactory.com/documents/al-saidi.pdf.

21. United States v. Narseal Batiste, U.S. government exhibits, 2006.

22. Tom Brune and James Ylisela Jr., "The Making of Jeff Fort," *Chicago Magazine*, November 1988.

23. United States v. Narseal Batiste, FBI transcripts, 2006.

24. Ibid.

25. United States v. Narseal Batiste, U.S. government exhibits, 2006.

26. United States v. Narseal Batiste, FBI transcripts, 2006.

27. Ibid.

28. Ibid.

29. Amanda Ripley, "Preemptive Terror Trials: Strike Two," *Time*, December 13, 2007.

30. United States v. Narseal Batiste, Trial transcripts, 2006.

31. United States v. Narseal Batiste, "Narseal Batiste's Supplement to Demand for Specific Kyles and Brady Information and Giglio/Napue Materials and Request For Expedited Ruling," August 27, 2007, http://theterrorfactory.com/documents/batiste398main.pdf.

32. Author interview with El Paso Police Department spokesman Darrel Petry, 2011.

4. LEVERAGE

1. Author interview with Foad Farahi, 2009.

2. Author interview with Ira Kurzban, 2009.

3. Author interview with Edward R. Sunshine, 2009.

4. Laura Wides-Munoz, "Illegal Immigrants Say They Were Targeted Because Daughter Is an Activist," *Associated Press*, April 8, 2008.

5. Eric Schmitt, "American Strike Is Said to Kill a Top Qaeda Leader," *New York Times*, May 31, 2010.

6. Pew Research Center for People and the Press, "Muslim Americans: No Signs of Growth in Alienation or Support for Extremism," August 30, 2011.

7. Mohammad Ayoub, "Study Shows Prospering Community," *Sun Sentinel*, November 14, 2005.

8. Charlie Savage, "F.B.I. Agents Get Leeway to Push Privacy Bounds," *New York Times*, June 12, 2011.

9. Sara Kehaulani Goo, "Sen. Kennedy Flagged by No-Fly List," *Washington Post*, August 20, 2004; Mimi Hall, "U.S. Has Mandela on Terrorist List," *USA Today*, April 30, 2008.

10. Author interview with Ibraheim Mashal, 2010.

11. Ayman Latif vs. Eric H. Holder, Jr., Complaint for injunctive

and declaratory relief, June 30, 2010, http://theterrorfactory.com/documents/latif-holder.pdf.

12. Author interview with Nusrat Choudhury, 2010.

13. Rob Wagner, "Alleged drug dealer faces kidnap charges," *San Gabriel Valley Tribune*, February 4, 1986.

14. Author interview with Craig Monteilh, 2011.

15. United States v. Tarek Mehanna, Affidavit, November 7, 2008, http://theterrorfactory.com/documents/mehanna_affidavit.pdf.

16. Nancy Murray, "It's Official. There Is a Muslim Exemption to the First Amendment," *Boston Globe*, April 12, 2012.

17. Andrew F. March, "A Dangerous Mind?" *New York Times*, April 21, 2012.

18. "Tarek's Sentencing Statement (with Leaked Voice and Subtitles)," video clip, YouTube, May 13, 2012, http://youtu.be/jtDReECm9oE!.

19. "Got Rights?" video clip, Muslim Advocates, http://muslimadvocates.org/get_involved/got_rights.html.

20. Author interview with Farhana Khera, 2011.

21. Pew Research Center for People and the Press, "Muslim Americans: No Signs of Growth in Alienation or Support for Extremism," August 30, 2011.

5. THE SUPERINFORMANT

1. Author interview with Mohammed Hossain, 2012.

2. United States v. James Cromitie, Trial transcripts, September 16, 2010, http://theterrorfactory.com/documents/cromitie_9-16-10.pdf, p. 1537; United States vs. James Cromitie, Trial transcripts, September 20, 2010, http://theterrorfactory.com/documents/cromitie_9-20-10.pdf, p. 1583.

3. United States v.. James Cromitie, Trial transcripts, September 16, 2010, http://theterrorfactory.com/documents/cromitie_9-16-10.pdf, p. 1542;United States v. James Cromitie, Trial transcripts, September 16, 2010, http://theterrorfactory.com/documents/cromitie_9-16-10.pdf, p. 1523.

4. United States v. James Cromitie, Trial transcripts, September 15, 2010, http://theterrorfactory.com/documents/

cromitie_9-15-10.pdf, Page 1269.

5. Ibid., p. 1214; Ibid, p. 1217.

6. Ibid., p. 1214.

7. Ibid., p. 1217-1218.

8. Ibid., p. 1219.

9. Ibid., p. 1220.

10. Ibid., p. 1221-1223.

11. United States v. James Cromitie, Trial transcripts, September 16, 2010, http://theterrorfactory.com/documents/cromitie_9-16-10.pdf, p. 1524.

12. United States v. James Cromitie, Trial transcripts, September 15, 2010, http://theterrorfactory.com/documents/cromitie_9-15-10.pdf, p. 1222.

13. Shahed Hussain, Voluntary petition, U.S. Bankruptcy Court Northern District of New York, August 21, 2003, http://theterrorfactory.com/documents/hussain_bankruptcy.pdf.

14. United States v. Yassin Aref, Trial transcripts, September 18, 2006, http://theterrorfactory.com/documents/aref_volume4.pdf, p. 463.

15. Ibid., p. 464.

16. Ibid., p. 466-467.

17. United States v. Shahed Hussain, Criminal complaint, January 2, 2002, http://theterrorfactory.com/documents/hussain_complaint.pdf.

18. United States v. Yassin Aref, Trial transcripts, September 18, 2006, http://theterrorfactory.com/documents/aref_volume4.pdf, p. 462.

19. United States v. James Cromitie, Trial transcripts, September 15, 2010, http://theterrorfactory.com/documents/cromitie_9-15-10.pdf, p. 1329.

20. Ibid., p. 2278.

21. Yassin Aref, *Son of Mountains*, The Troy Book Makers, 2008.

22. Federal Bureau of Investigation, Investigation reports, January 2004, http://theterrorfactory.com/documents/albany_fbi_reports.pdf.

23. Yassin Aref file, Federal Bureau of Investigation, http://theterrorfactory.com/documents/aref_foipa.pdf.

24. United States v. Yassin Aref, Trial transcripts, September 14, 2006, http://theterrorfactory.com/documents/aref_volume2.pdf, p. 301.

25. Ibid., p. 835.

26. Author interview with Kathy Manley, 2010.

27. Federal Bureau of Investigation, Video transcripts, January 2, 2004, http://theterrorfactory.com/documents/albany_video_1-2-04.pdf.

28. Wesley Yang, "The Terrorist Search Engine," *New York Magazine,* December 5, 2010.

29. Vanessa Blum, "Terror Analyst's Credentials Questioned," *Sun Sentinel*, August 27, 2006; Matthew Barakat, "Defense Seeks to Bar Testimony from 'Doogie Howser' of Terrorism," *Associated Press*, March 17, 2005; Brendan J. Lyons, "Lawyer Looks to Block Witness; Controversial Terrorism Expert's Credentials Questioned by Defense," *Times Union*, September 27, 2006.

30. Yang, "The Terrorist Search Engine."

31. Richard B. Schmitt, "Antiterror Expertise Goes High-Tech: Many Consultants Young, Web-Savvy," *Boston Globe*, April 25, 2004.

32. Investigative Project on Terrorism, IRS Form 990, August 11, 2011, http://theterrorfactory.com/documents/iptf990.pdf.

33. United States v. Yassin Aref, Affirmation in support of motion, September 26, 2004, http://theterrorfactory.com/documents/aref_motion.pdf.

34. Robert Gavin, "Terror Convictions Put to the Test; Convicted in 2006 After a Fictitious Plot, 2 Members of an Albany Mosque Take Case to Federal Appeals Court," *Times Union*, March 25, 2008.

35. United States v. Yassin Aref, Trial transcripts, September 18, 2006, http://theterrorfactory.com/documents/aref_volume4.pdf, p. 630.

36. United States v. James Cromitie, Trial transcripts, September 16, 2010, http://theterrorfactory.com/documents/cromitie_9-16-10.pdf, p. 1511.

37. United States v. James Cromitie, Trial transcripts, September 23, 2010, http://theterrorfactory.com/documents/

cromitie_9-23-10.pdf, p. 2343.

38. United States v. James Cromitie, Trial transcripts, September 16, 2010, http://theterrorfactory.com/documents/cromitie_9-16-10. pdf, p. 1471.

39. United States v. James Cromitie, Trial transcripts, September 16, 2010, http://theterrorfactory.com/documents/cromitie_9-16-10. pdf, p. 1489.

40. United States v. James Cromitie, Trial transcripts, September 16, 2010, http://theterrorfactory.com/documents/cromitie_9-16-10. pdf, p. 1407.

41. Michelle Shephard and Tonda MacCharles, "Khadr linked Arar to terrorism, court hears," *Toronto Star*, January 19, 2009.

42. United States v. James Cromitie, Trial transcripts, September 23, 2010, http://theterrorfactory.com/documents/cromitie_9-23-10. pdf, p. 2343.

43. Ibid., p. 2298.

44. New York State Parole Board, Hearing transcript, August 6, 1991, http://theterrorfactory.com/documents/cromitie_parole.pdf.

45. United States v. James Cromitie, Trial transcripts, September 16, 2010, http://theterrorfactory.com/documents/cromitie_9-16-10. pdf, p. 1400.

46. United States v. James Cromitie, FBI undercover transcript, November 14, 2008, http://theterrorfactory.com/documents/ cromitie_undercover1.pdf, p. 72.

47. United States v. James Cromitie, FBI undercover transcript, October 19, 2008, http://theterrorfactory.com/documents/cromitie_ undercover1.pdf, p. 20.

48. United States v. James Cromitie, Trial transcripts, September 20, 2010, http://theterrorfactory.com/documents/cromitie_9-20-10. pdf, p. 1678-1679.

49. United States v. James Cromitie, FBI undercover transcript, November 29, 2008, http://theterrorfactory.com/documents/ cromitie_undercover1.pdf, p. 121.

50. United States v. James Cromitie, Trial transcripts, September 21, 2010, http://theterrorfactory.com/documents/cromitie_9-21-10. pdf, p. 1869.

51. Ibid., p. 1960.

52. United States v. James Cromitie, Trial transcripts, September 8, 2010, http://theterrorfactory.com/documents/cromitie_9-8-10.pdf, p. 1021.

53. United States v. James Cromitie, Trial transcripts, September 21, 2010, http://theterrorfactory.com/documents/cromitie_9-21-10.pdf, p. 1857.

54. United States v. James Cromitie, FBI undercover transcript, April 16, 2009, http://theterrorfactory.com/documents/cromitie_undercover2.pdf, p. 89.

55. United States v. James Cromitie, Trial transcripts, September 16, 2010, http://theterrorfactory.com/documents/cromitie_9-16-10.pdf, p. 1408.

56. United States v. James Cromitie, FBI undercover transcript, April 7, 2009, http://theterrorfactory.com/documents/cromitie_undercover2.pdf, p. 74.

57. United States v. James Cromitie, FBI undercover transcript, April 23, 2009, http://theterrorfactory.com/documents/cromitie_undercover2.pdf, p. 151.

58. United States v. James Cromitie, Trial transcripts, August 25, 2010, http://theterrorfactory.com/documents/cromitie_8-25-10.pdf, p. 300.

59. "4 Muslims Arrested: NYC Jewish Temple Bomb Plots," video clip, May 20, 2009, YouTube, http://youtu.be/kI3Y1qVA4F8.

60. Chris Dolmetsch and Patricia Hurtado, "New York City Synagogue Bomb Plotters Are Sentenced to 25 Years in Prison," *Bloomberg*, June 29, 2011.

6. "TO CATCH THE DEVIL, YOU HAVE TO GO TO HELL"

1. Andrew Blankstein and Richard Serrano, "Whitey Bulger Arrest: FBI Agents seize $800,000 in Cash, Arsenal of Weapons from Santa Monica Apartment," *Los Angeles Times*, June 23, 2011.

2. Tonya Alanez, "Man Jailed for 6 Years Takes Plea Deal for Shooting Death," *Sun Sentinel*, January 15, 2010.

3. Steve Miletich and Mike Carter, "Violent Criminal on Federal Payroll as Informant," *Seattle Times*, April 16, 2012.

4. "United States Attorneys' Annual Statistical Report," U.S. Department of Justice, 2011, http://theterrorfactory.com/

documents/11statrpt.pdf.

5. William Glaberson, "Terror Case Hinges on a Wobbly Key Player," *New York Times*, November 27, 2004.

6. Indictment, United States v. Mohammed Ali Hassan Al-Moayad, December 13, 2004, http://theterrorfactory.com/documents/al-moayad_indictment.pdf.

7. James Irmas, "Year of the Rats," *Village Voice*, February 5, 2008.

8. Criminal complaint, United States v. Tarik Ibn Osman Shah, May 27, 2005, http://theterrorfactory.com/documents/shah_complaint.pdf.

9. Alan Feuer, "Tapes Capture Bold Claims of Bronx Man in Terror Plot," *New York Times*, May 8, 2007.

10. Alan Feuer, "Bronx Man Pleads Guilty in Terror Case," *New York Times*, April 5, 2007.

11. Author interview with Marlene Jenkins, 2011.

12. Caryle Murphy and Del Quentin Wilber, "Terror Informant Ignites Himself Near White House," *Washington Post*, November 16, 2004.

13. John Marzulli, "Suicidal Tipster: Cleric Gave Osama $20m," *New York Daily News*, February 18, 2005.

14. Leo Strupczewski, "N.J. Man Thought Little of His Terror Tip," *Courier-Post*, May 29, 2007.

15. Criminal complaint, United States v. Dritan Duka, May 7, 2007, http://theterrorfactory.com/documents/duka_complaint.pdf.

16. "Fort Dix Witness Cites Terrorism Threat," *United Press International*, December 10, 2008.

17. Excerpt from court transcripts, United States v. Mohamad Ibrahim Shnewer, http://theterrorfactory.com/documents/fortdix413.pdf.

18. Sentencing memorandum, United States v. Derrick Shareef, September 26, 2008, http://theterrorfactory.com/documents/shareef_sentencing.pdf.

19. Criminal complaint, United States v. Derrick Shareef, December 8, 2006, http://theterrorfactory.com/documents/shareef_complaint.pdf.

20. Mike Robinson, "Man charged in plot to bomb Rockford mall," *Associated Press*, December 8, 2006.

21. Criminal complaint, United States v. Michael C. Finton, September 24, 2009, http://theterrorfactory.com/documents/finton_complaint.pdf.

22. Ibid.

23. Affidavit, United States v. Rezwan Ferdaus, September 28, 2011, http://theterrorfactory.com/documents/ferdaus_affidavit.pdf.

24. David Boeri, "At Hearing, Informant Under Fire in Ashland Terror Plot Case," WBUR, November 15, 2011.

25. Denise Lavoie, "Rezwan Ferdaus Admits Guilt in Plot to Blow Up Pentagon and U.S. Capitol," *Associated Press*, July 20, 2012.

26. Susan Kelleher and Steve Miletich, "Suspect's Troubled Past: Rap Sheet, Hallucinations," *Seattle Times*, June 24, 2011.

27. Author interview with Michele Shaw, 2011.

28. Susan Kelleher, "Suspect's Life Marked by Mental Illness, Acquaintance Says," *Seattle Times*, June 24, 2011.

29. Janet I. Tu, "Wife of Man Accused of Terrorist Plot: 'He Is Not an Extremist,'" *Seattle Times*, June 24, 2011.

30. Levi Pulkkinen, "Key Witness in Seattle Terror Plot Was Sex Offender," *Seattle Post-Intelligencer*, July 26, 2012.

31. Abu Khalid Abdul-Latif, Voluntary Petition, U.S. Bankruptcy Court, May 20, 2011, http://theterrorfactory.com/documents/latif_bankruptcy.pdf.

32. Criminal complaint, United States v. Abu Khalid Abdul-Latif, June 23, 2011, http://theterrorfactory.com/documents/latif_complaint.pdf.

33. Levi Pulkkinen, "Key Witness in Seattle Terror Plot Was Sex Offender," *Seattle Post-Intelligencer*, July 26, 2012.

7. NOT CAUGHT ON TAPE

1. Memorandum in Support of Motion to Suppress the Products of Non-FISA Interrogations, Searches, and Seizures, United States v. Mohamed Osmon Mohamud, June 22, 2011, http://theterrorfactory.com/documents/mohamud_6-22-11.pdf.

2. Ibid.

3. Paul Cruickshank, "U.S. Citizen Believed to Be Writing for Al Qaeda Website, Source Says," CNN, July 18, 2010.

4. Damien McElroy, Adrian Blomfield and Nasser Arrabyee,

"Anwar al-Awlaki: Drone Kills US-Born Preacher Who Inspired Lone Wolf Terrorists," *Telegraph*, September 30, 2011.

5. Criminal complaint, United States v. Mohamed Osmon Mohamud, November 26, 2010, http://theterrorfactory.com/documents/mohamud_complaint.pdf.

6. "FBI Sting Foils Portland Terror Plot," video clip, Nov. 27, 2010, YouTube, http://youtu.be/pGYj6FnNTMk.

7. Criminal complaint, U.S. vs. Antonio Martinez, December 8, 2010, http://theterrorfactory.com/documents/martinez_complaint.pdf.

8. United States v. James Cromitie, Trial transcripts, September 16, 2010, http://theterrorfactory.com/documents/cromitie_9-16-10.pdf, p. 1539.

9. Criminal complaint, United States v. Abu Khalid Abdul-Latif, June 23, 2011, http://theterrorfactory.com/documents/latif_complaint.pdf.

10. Aaron C. Davis, "Judge Sentences Lodi man to 24 Years for Attending Terror Camp," *Associated Press*, September 10, 2007.

11. Lowell Bergman and Oriana Zill de Granados, "The Enemy Within," PBS *Frontline*, October 10, 2006.

12. Rone Tempest, "Lodi Man Describes Terrorist Training," *Los Angeles Times*, March 8, 2006.

13. The Center on Law and Security, New York University School of Law, "TTRC Update: Informant Cases and the Entrapment Defense," March 2011.

8. MISSION ACCOMPLISHED

1. "FY 2012 Budget Request at a Glance," Federal Bureau of Investigation, http://theterrorfactory.com/documents/fy2012budget.pdf.

2. Robert S. Mueller III, "Before the Senate Committee on the Judiciary Washington, DC," Federal Bureau of Investigation, January 20, 2010.

3. "2003 State of the Union," video clip, January 28, 2003, C-SPAN, http://www.c-spanvideo.org/program/174799-2.

4. Lowell Bergman and Matthew Purdy, "Chasing the Sleeper Cell," PBS *Frontline*, October 16, 2003.

5. Lou Michel, "U.S. Gives Half of the Lackawanna Six a Fresh Start," *Buffalo News*, August 20, 2010.

6. "Press Briefing on Miami Terror Indictments," Transcript, CNN, June 23, 2006.

7. "Headlines - The Apprentices," video clip, June 26, 2006, *The Daily Show*, http://www.thedailyshow.com/watch/mon-june-26-2006/headlines---the-apprentices.

8. "Attorney General Eric Holder Speaks at the Muslim Advocates' Annual Dinner," Department of Justice, December 10, 2010, http://theterrorfactory.com/documents/HolderSpeechDec2010.pdf.

9. "Government's Response to Defendant's Motion for Order Directing the Government to Cease and Desist from Inappropriate Pretrial Comment," United States v. Mohamed Osman Mohamud, January 10, 2011, http://theterrorfactory.com/documents/mohamud_doc20.pdf.

10. Email originally obtained by reporter Josh Bernstein.

11. "Home Grown Terror? FBI: Plots Foiled in Two States," ABC News, September 25, 2009.

12. "Criminal Complaint," United States v. Hosam Maher Husein Smadi, September 24, 2009, http://theterrorfactory.com/documents/smadi_complaint.pdf.

13. "Indictment," United States v. Farooque Ahmed, October 26, 2010, http://theterrorfactory.com/documents/ahmed_indictment.pdf.

14. "Taborn on Arrest of Farooque Ahmed," video clip, YouTube, October 27, 2010, http://www.youtube.com/watch?v=JmyJO5Pue4I.

15. Justin Elliott, "Fact-Check: How the NYPD Overstated Its Counterterrorism Record," ProPublica, July 10, 2012.

16. Jerry Markon, "Post-9/11 Probe Revived Stolen-Cereal Incident," *Washington Post*, June 15, 2005.

9. ONE MAN'S TERRORIST, ANOTHER MAN'S FOOL

1. Richard Lord, "Accused Local Taliban Sympathizer Detained Without Bond Until Trial," *Pittsburgh Post-Gazette*, March 16, 2012.

2. Dane Schiller, "Accused Terrorist Secretly Recorded Talking

Jihad," *Houston Chronicle*, November 9, 2011.

3. U.S. Department of Homeland Security, "Rightwing Extremism: Current Economic and Political Climate Fueling Resurgence in Radicalization and Recruitment," April 7, 2009, http://theterrorfactory.com/documents/rightwing.pdf

4. FoxNews.com, "Chorus of Protest Grows Over Report Warning of Right Wing Radicalization", April 15, 2009, http://www.foxnews.com/politics/2009/04/15/chorus-protest-grows-report-warning-right-wing-radicalization/

5. "RAW VIDEO: West Memphis Shooting," video clip, YouTube, June 30, 2010, http://youtu.be/acLpCbbZ1fk.

6. J.J. MacNab, " 'Sovereign' Citizen Kane," *Intelligence Report*, Fall 2010.

7. Author interview with Bob Paudert, 2012.

8. Kristina Goetz, "No Hints at Violence in Sovereign Citizen Jerry Kane's File," *Commercial Appeal*, May 20, 12.

9. FBI Law Enforcement Bulletin, "Sovereign Citizens: A Growing Domestic Threat to Law Enforcement," September 2011, http://www.fbi.gov/stats-services/publications/law-enforcement-bulletin/september-2011/sovereign-citizens

10. Bob Willis, "U.S. Recession Worst Since Great Depression, Revised Data Show," *Bloomberg*, August 1, 2009.

11. Adam H. Beasley, "Florida: A Ponzi Schemer's Paradise," *Miami Herald*, July 7, 2012.

12. David K. Shipler, "Terrorist Plots, Hatched by the F.B.I.," *New York Times*, April 28, 2012.

13. Rick Lyman and Nick Madigan, "Officials Puzzled About Motive of Airport Gunman Who Killed 2," *New York Times*, July 6, 2002; William K. Rashbaum, "Terror Suspect Is Charged with Preparing Explosives," *New York Times*, September 25, 2009; William K. Rashbaum, Mark Mazzetti, and Peter Baker, "Owner of S.U.V. Arrested in Times Sq. Bomb Case," *New York Times*, May 4, 2010.

14. Paul Finkelman, "John Brown: America's First Terrorist?" *Prologue Magazine*, Spring 2011.

INDEX